Native American Literature

Twayne's United States Authors Series

Warren French, Editor

Indiana University, Indianapolis

TUSAS 467

"Storytelling Woman"
by Wendy Rose

Native American Literature

By Andrew Wiget

New Mexico State University

Twayne Publishers • *Boston*

Native American Literature

Andrew Wiget

Copyright © 1985 by G. K. Hall & Company
All Rights Reserved
Published by Twayne Publishers
A Division of G. K. Hall & Co.
70 Lincoln Street
Boston, Massachusetts 02111

Book production by Elizabeth Todesco

Book design by Barbara Anderson

Printed on permanent/durable acid-free
paper and bound in the United States of
America.

Library of Congress Cataloging in Publication Data

Wiget, Andrew.
  Native American literature.

  (Twayne's United States authors series: TUSAS 467)
  Bibliography: p. 135
  Includes index.
  1. Indian literature—North America—History and criticism.
2. American literature—Indian authors—History and criticism.
I. Title. II. Series.
PM155.W54   1985   810'.9'897   84-19809
ISBN 0-8057-7408-4

Contents

About the Author

Andrew Wiget, currently assistant professor of English at New Mexico State University, received the Ph.D. from the University of Utah in 1977, after having written both his thesis and dissertation on Native American oral literatures. Besides numerous reviews in the field, he has published articles on Zuni, Aztec, Eskimo, and Navajo oral literature, on nineteenth and twentieth century Indian writers, and on the teaching of Native American literature, an activity that has occupied him for the last ten years. He has coauthored a volume on the history of the Utah Navajo, contributed to an MLA-sponsored study of American Indian literature, and served as an officer of the Association for the Study of American Indian Literatures. His *Critical Essays on Native American Literature* is also published by G. K. Hall.

Preface

The verbal skill of Native Americans was known to the first Europeans and evoked from Thomas Jefferson comparisons to the classical authors of Rome whom he admired so much. By the turn of this century, their accomplishments in English were also widely admired. Formal recognition of cultural as well as individual achievement came in 1969, when N. Scott Momaday, a Kiowa author and professor of comparative literature, was awarded the Pulitzer Prize for his novel *House Made of Dawn*. Yet for all this literary production, there has been no single effort to order and assess this literature, and so this book was conceived. In this effort, I have allowed myself the broadest possible latitude in definition, including when useful literature from the Arctic, Canada, and Mesoamerica, in the belief that a harmony of perspectives exists within the cultural pluralism of Native America that transcends postinvasion political boundaries. Tribal synonymy being a perpetual problem, I have conformed to the usage found in Murdock and O'Leary's *Ethnographic Bibliography* except where authors have indicated their own preferences for native-language tribal names (e.g., Vizenor, Anishinabe instead of Chippewa).

Because of the importance of the long tribal tradition of orally transmitted literature to Native American culture, the first two chapters of this book are devoted to these works: the first to oral narratives, especially creation myths, and the second to oratory and poetry, including that used in rituals. The third chapter discusses the beginnings in the eighteenth and nineteenth centuries of a literature written in English by Indian authors, who produced religious and political writings, autobiographies, and early lyric poetry and fiction. Chapters 4 and 5 survey, respectively, recent achievements in Native American fiction and poetry, while the final chapter glances briefly at the latest ventures of Native American writers into such other forms as nonfictional prose, autobiographical narrative, and drama.

I would like to acknowledge here those whose advice, assistance, and collegial interest have been in great part responsible for the virtues of this book. The MLA Seminar on American Indian Literature in Flagstaff (1977), coordinated by Larry Evers of the University of Arizona and Paula Gunn Allen, and the NEH Summer Seminar on Oral Literature (1980), directed by Richard Bauman at the University of Texas–Austin, were invaluable postgraduate experiences. My former colleague in Dartmouth's Native American Studies Program, Michael Green, generously read and commented on portions of the manuscript. The Dartmouth Committee on Faculty Research provided funds for research materials and manuscript preparation, and Terry Hall, Frances Dupuis, and Lucie Minsk typed the final text diligently and with good humor. A special thanks to Wendy Rose for providing her drawing, *Storytelling Woman,* for the frontispiece of this volume.

My wife, Cathy, and my children, Sarah and Paul, patiently endured their roles as book-widow and book-orphans, and in the end provided me with as much motivation to finish the book as they had to start it.

Andrew Wiget

New Mexico State University

Acknowledgments

The author is grateful to the following authors and publishers for permission to use copyrighted material:

Joy Harjo for lines from "For Alva Benson and All Those Who Learned to Speak," unpublished, and Joy Harjo and Ishmael Reed Books (Reed and Cannon Communications Co., 2140 Shattuck Avenue, Suite 11, Berkeley, CA 94704) for poetry from *What Moon Drove Me to This?* by Joy Harjo, © 1969 by Joy Harjo. Harper & Row Publishers, Inc., for lines from *House Made of Dawn* by N. Scott Momaday, © 1966, 1967, 1968 by N. Scott Momaday; *The Gourd Dancer* by N. Scott Momaday, © 1976, by N. Scott Momaday; from *Going For the Rain* by Simon J. Ortiz, © 1976 by Simon J. Ortiz; from *Riding the Earthboy 40* by James Welch, © 1971, 1976 by James Welch; from *Winter of the Salamander* by Ray Young Bear, © 1980 by Ray Young Bear; from *Ascending Red Cedar Moon* by Duane Niatum, © 1973 by Duane Niatum; from *Digging Out the Roots* by Duane Niatum, © 1978 by Duane Niatum. Lance Henson for lines from *Mistah* © 1977 by Lance Henson. Linda Hogan for lines from *Calling Myself Home,* © 1978 by Linda Hogan, and *Daughters, I Love You,* © 1981 by Linda Hogan and The Research Center for Women, Loretto Heights College. Maurice Kenny for lines from *Dancing Back Strong the Nation* © 1979, and *Kneading the Blood* by Maurice Kenny, © 1981. Simon J. Ortiz for lines from *From Sand Creek,* by Simon J. Ortiz, © 1981 by Simon J. Ortiz. Wendy Rose, Strawberry Press, and Malki Museum Press for lines from *Long Division: A Tribal History,* © 1976 by Wendy Rose; Wendy Rose and Malki Museum Press for lines from *Academic Squaw: Reports to the World from the Ivory Tower* by Wendy Rose, © 1977 by Wendy Rose, and from *Builder Kachina: A Home-Going Cycle,* by Wendy Rose, © 1979 by Wendy Rose; and Wendy Rose for the frontispiece in this volume. University of New Mexico Press for lines from Leslie Silko's "Bear Country" in *The Remembered Earth* by Geary Hobson, © 1981 by the University of New Mexico Press. University of Oklahoma Press for "Indian Reservations in the 'Lower 48,' 1969" (Map) from *A History of the Indians of the United States,* by Angie Debo, © 1970 by the University of Oklahoma Press. University of Utah Press for lines from translation of Aztec poetry in *Grammatical Examples, Exercises and Review for use with Rules of the Aztec Language,* by Arthur J.O. Anderson, ©

Chronology

50,000 B.C. Native Americans bring shamanic religion and core Earth-Diver and Trickster myths to North America.

7,000 B.C. Emergence myth develops in conjunction with agriculture in Mesoamerica.

1560s Fray Bernardino de Sahagun records Aztec oral literature.

1665 Caleb Chaesahteamuk (Natick), the first Native American college graduate, leaves Harvard Indian College (fd. 1656), fluent in Latin, Greek, and English.

1680 The Pueblo Revolt drives the Spanish from New Mexico for twelve years.

1772 Samson Occum (Mohegan) publishes his "Sermon on the Execution of Moses Paul . . ." and his *Choice Collection of Hymns and Spiritual Songs* (1774), first works in English by a Native American.

1790 Through Trade and Intercourse Acts, the United States government asserts sole responsibility for relations with Indian nations as foreign sovereignties.

1823 *Poor Sarah . . .*, by Elias Boudinot (Cherokee), a fictionalized conversion story, possibly first Native American fiction.

1824 Office of Indian Affairs created in War Department; moved as Bureau to new Department of Interior in 1849.

1827 David Cusick (Tuscarora) publishes *Ancient History of the Six Nations,* first historical work by Native American author.

1829 William Apes (Pequot) publishes *A Son of the Forest,* the first autobiography written by a Native American.

1831–1832 The United States Supreme Court, in "the Cherokee cases," affirms sovereignty of Indian tribes as "domestic dependent nations."

1833 The first "as-told-to" autobiography, that of Black Hawk (Sauk), is published.

1837   President Andrew Jackson begins enforcing the Indian Removal Act of 1830, driving southern tribes on Trail of Tears across the Mississippi River.

1854   John Rollin Ridge (Cherokee) publishes fictional *Life and Adventures of Joaquin Murieta*.

1868   The same Ridge's *Poems* becomes the first volume of poetry published by a Native American.

1871   Congress ends treaty-making; refuses to recognize Indian tribes as independent nations.

1876   Custer defeated at Little Bighorn.

1879   Bureau of American Ethnology established to study native cultures.

1885   Daniel Crane Brinton begins publishing Library of Aboriginal Literature aimed at preserving "classics" of Native American oral literature.

1887   The General Allotment (Dawes) Act, aimed at the assimilation of Native Americans by subdividing and individually assigning communal reservation land.

1890   Massacre of Ghost Dancers at Wounded Knee, S.D.

1899   *Queen of the Woods,* novel, published posthumously by Simon Pokagon (Potowatomi).

1902   Charles Eastman (Yankton Sioux) publishes *Indian Boyhood,* followed by *The Soul of an Indian* (1911).

1924   Indian Voting Rights Act.

1934   The Indian Reorganization (Wheeler-Howard) Act provides means for tribal self-government.

1936   D'Arcy McNickle (Salish) publishes *The Surrounded.*

1946   Congress establishes Indian Claims Commission.

1953   House C.R. 108 directs "termination" of Federal-Indian trust relationship; policy later reversed.

1969   N. Scott Momaday (Kiowa) wins Pulitzer Prize for novel *House Made of Dawn;* special issue of *South Dakota Review,* "The American Indian Speaks."

1973   Occupation of Wounded Knee, S.D., by AIM members.

1974   *Winter in the Blood,* by James Welch (Blackfeet/Gros

Ventre), hailed in *New York Times* as "best first novel of the season."

1975   *Carriers of the Dream Wheel,* first substantial collection of contemporary Native American poetry.

1977   Leslie Silko (Laguna) publishes widely acclaimed novel *Ceremony;* awarded prestigious MacArthur Foundation Fellowship in 1981 for her achievement.

Chapter One
Oral Narrative

Archaeologists have long argued that Native Americans arrived from Asia in successive waves over several millennia, crossing a lush flowered plain hundreds of miles wide that now lies inundated by 160 feet of water released by melting glaciers. For several periods of time, the first beginning around 60,000 B.C. and the last ending around 7000 B.C., the land bridge now known as Beringia was open. The first people came earlier than 30,000 B.C., traveling in the dusty trails of the animals they hunted, unaware of the historical consequence of their daily routine.[1] They brought with them not only their families, weapons, and tools, but a broad metaphysical understanding, sprung from dreams and visions and articulated in myth and song, which complemented their scientific and historical knowledge of the lives of animals and of men. All this they caught up, shaped carefully and deliberately in a variety of languages, bringing into being oral literatures of power and beauty, and so coming into possession of themselves in the land that was beginning to possess them.

Contemporary readers, forgetting the origins of Western epic, lyric, and dramatic forms, are easily disposed to think of "literature" only as something written. But upon reflection it quickly becomes clear that the more critically useful as well as the more frequently employed sense of the term concerns the artfulness of the verbal creation, not its mode of presentation. Ultimately literature is aesthetically valued, regardless of language, culture, or mode of presentation, because some significant verbal achievement results from the struggle in words between tradition and talent. As an accomplished Inuit singer told the Danish polar explorer Knud Rasmussen, "the most festive thing of all is joy in beautiful, smooth words and our ability to express them."[2] What one seeks, then is verbal art, the ability to shape out a compelling inner vision in some skillfully crafted public verbal form.

Performance, Form, and Genre

Of course, the differences between the written and oral modes of expression are not without consequences for an understanding of Native American literature. Because the modalities have different capacities, precisely the opposite is true. The essential difference is that a speech event is an evolving communication, an "emergent form,"[3] the shape, functions, and aesthetic values of which become more clearly realized over the course of the performance. In performing verbal art, the performer assumes responsibility before the audience for the manner as well as the content of the performance, while the audience assumes the responsibility throughout for evaluating the performer's competence in both areas. It is this intense mutual engagement that elicits the display of skill and shapes the emerging performance. Where written literature provides us with a tradition of texts, oral literature offers a tradition of performances. In both cases, however, the art lies not in the modality itself but in the effective use of its possibilities within culturally defined aesthetic norms.

Traditional folkloric studies of Native American oral literature worked with transcriptions of the verbal component of the performance, as if those "texts" represented the reality. But transcribing an oral performance is, to borrow Albert Lord's phrase, like "photographing Proteus,"[4] and immediately produces an anomaly that is neither a part of a living folkloric tradition nor of a truly literary one. Consequently, literary criticism of Native American oral literatures founded on a conventional notion of text and evolved from analogies to Western genres, styles, and aesthetic values soon proves of little value. Written texts, the object of literary criticism, are composed entirely of printed linguistic signs, but, as Judith Irvine has recently pointed out, linguistic complexity is only one dimension of form in a speech event. She observes that formality may be heightened in a speech event not only by increasing the number of rules governing what is appropriate language but by increasing correlation between verbal and nonverbal aspects of the event; by increasing the prominence given to one's social, as opposed to personal, identity; and by increasing the centralization of space in which the event occurs.[5] Only the first of these is applicable to written literature.

One of the differences between narrative and song, for instance, is the addition of more rules governing expression (metrical rules: prosody; semantic rules: figurative language; structural rules) and the correlation of two modes of expression, verbal and tonal. Similarly, the difference between conversation and oratory has to do not only with the participants' shift from private identity to public role but also to an increasingly centralized focus for the event. It may be possible, then, to suggest distinctions in terms of several kinds of formality, acknowledging, of course, that such distinctions are necessarily abstracted from the particular situation in an individual community, where additional distinguishing features may be involved. One might begin with narrative as the form more often than not the least structured textually and contextually. Oratory and lyric song are intermediate forms; lyric song may be more structured linguistically than all kinds of oratory, but oratory of all kinds is almost always more structured contextually. Ritual chant and song are often the most structured forms in all ways. The present chapter will examine narrative forms of Native American verbal art, while the second will address oratory and both ritual and lyric song.

From the beginning, trying to find some clear and universal criteria for distinguishing different types of narratives has been the ever-elusive goal of folklorists and anthropologists. Alan Dundes demonstrated that such a goal was unattainable when he concluded a study of Native American stories by announcing that "myth and folktale are not structurally distinct genres . . . . The distinction between them is wholly dependent upon content criteria or totally external factors such as belief or function. Thus [Franz] Boas was basically correct in distinguishing myths from folktales on the basis of content differences such as setting, time, and dramatis personae."[6] In effect, Dundes acknowledged that what distinguishes these stories for Native Americans was not comprehended by his analysis at all, each tribe having instead its own criteria. Based on a widespread Native American sense of narrative time,[7] however, it is possible to make some cross-cultural generalizations and still acknowledge elements of setting that are important features in these tribal genres. In the progress of narrative time, the principal figures are a series of mediators who incarnate supernatural power and values in the present moment, thus communicating prototypical realities to each succeeding new world. In this way cultural institutions come to be understood as both created, historical realities and yet images of eternal verities. In this perspective, the sequence of narrative forms reconstructs a native consciousness of the narrated past (see Figure 1).

The past begins in the Origin Period. In some cultures the most remotely conceptualized being is an Asexual Spiritual Being like the Aztec Ometeotl, whose dynamic self-reflection creates through thought emanation either two Sky Parents Proper (Sun Father, Moon Mother) or Displaced (Sky Father, Earth Mother). Their intercourse creates two worlds (Mountain, Water; East, West; Zenith, Nadir) requiring reconciliation. This movement of mediation can be envisioned either as an Ascent (Emergence) or a Descent (Earth-Diver). At the point of Emergence or Contact there appears a mediational figure like the Seneca Woman Who

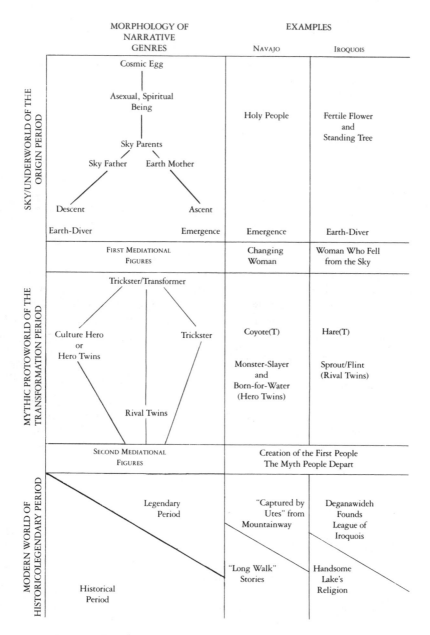

Figure 1. Native American Oral Narrative Genres

Fell from the Sky, the Navajo Changing Woman, or the Maidu Earth-Initiate, whose incarnation begins the birthing of spiritual power into the present, earth-surface world, and whose body upon decease sometimes becomes the first plants and animals.

Responsibility for further creation is then passed on in the Transformation Period. In some cases responsibility is given to a single figure whose character incarnates the polar values of Culture Hero and Trickster. This person may remain an integrated Trickster/Transformer or have the power to transform itself into either pole; hence, the Algonkian Manabozho as Culture Hero and as Trickster, Hare. Where the Trickster is undifferentiated from the Transformer, responsibility for further transformation can be given to demiurgic Twins who are themselves polar opposites, like the Seneca Rival Twins, Flint (Hunting) and Sprout (Agriculture), or the Navajo Hero Twins, Monster-Slayer (Active, Warrior) and Born-for-Water (Passive, Shaman). In any case, all three roles may coexist in a single character, although the tasks of the Transformer and Culture Hero are logically, if not chronologically, prior to those of the Trickster, for the sober implication of Trickster's buffoonery is that man's power in the world is finally limited. As the Transformation Period closes, the mediational figure creates the first real men and, in creating their clans, the first social structure. In many cultures these functions are achieved during the course of a migration.

The presence of men and of historically recognizable social structures and settings marks the Legendary/Historical Period. During this period sacred power remains active in places and things but its personal agents have removed themselves, leaving only ritual heroes and shamans as mediating agents. The heroes of the Legendary Period are the first men and women to avail themselves of these powers. The Legendary merges with the Historical as the sacred power quest pattern of legendary heroes becomes impressed upon the adventures of the secular hero. With the Historical Period, concern is turned away from acquiring wholly new forms of spiritual power to maintaining conventional channels.

The Earth-Diver Myth Complex

The Earth-Diver myth has wide distribution throughout North America, where it appears prominently in native literatures everywhere except in the Southwest, the Southeast, the Northwest Coast, and the Arctic. Even in these areas, however, important elements of the myth occur singly or in combination with motifs from the locally more common Emergence myth.

The myth is further distributed throughout Asia and Europe from Siberia to the Balkans and from Scandinavia to the Near East, where it has frequently been accommodated to the major "book" religions. This circumpolar distribution and the occurrence of the Earth-Diver elements in origin myths of clearly later invention suggest the myth's great age, even that it may have come to this continent with the first Paleolithic hunters who settled in the northern forests and eastern woodlands.

The myth has been summarized succinctly by Reichard: "A flood occurs—either a primeval flood or a deluge with various causes given. A few animals survive, usually on a raft on the surface of the waters. They feel the necessity for having land. A number of them dive for it, but come to the surface dead. A final attempt is made, often by Muskrat; and the successful animal appears exhausted but carrying mud in mouth, ears, nails, paws, and armpits. The dirt magically becomes larger until the whole earth is restored. The increased size is often brought about by running round and round the bit of land."[8] Yet the Earth-Diver myth cannot be so narrowly circumscribed. Reichard herself acknowledges its close links to several other important myths. And such a simple summary, by violating the poetic and dramatic power of the myth's several distinctive versions, would suggest that the story has only an explanatory function. In fact, in its full imaginative realization if not in its outline, the Earth-Diver myth compels one to imagine eternity. That is as much a storyteller's as a philosopher's problem.

In one telling, alone in the middle of a vast sea limned in darkness, a small raft bobbed. In the Arapaho version it contained a man, a woman, and a boy. For the Tlingit the raft was a bed of kelp and supported Raven the Trickster, who woke to find himself cast down from eternity at the beginning of time. For northern Athabascan peoples like the Kutchin of Canada's Mackenzie-Yukon region, the raft contained Crow the Trickster and other animals. When mud was brought up by Muskrat, Crow thrust his cane through it, planting it securely; on it the world began to grow. The Maidu of California believe that the raft, drifting in darkness out of the north, bore only two persons, Turtle and Father-of-Secret-Society. Suddenly a rope was let down in front of them. As the two peered up the rope into the darkness, a point of light emerged and grew larger as it drew nearer, until the figure of Earth-Initiate, his face covered but his body radiant as the sun, stepped into the bow of the boat and filled the world with light. After he agreed with Turtle that man should be created, Turtle weighted himself with a stone and plunged to the bottom of the ocean to bring up a bit of mud from which the dry earth would be made. Four times Earth-Initiate caused it to expand, until the raft ran aground on the shore of history.[9]

The Iroquoian version begins in a Skyworld encampment in form and population not unlike the Iroquois' own, except that the only light radiates from the blossoms of a tree planted in the center of the camp.[10] The Sky-woman, by another name the "Fertile Flower," marries Standing Tree, the chief of the Skyworld and owner of the Tree of Light. After their marriage their commingling breath causes her to become pregnant, but Standing Tree, knowing only that he has not had sexual intercourse with her, is unable to comprehend the magical cause of her condition and becomes jealous. He holds a dream feast to discern the outcome of the problem. In his dreaming he sees that all growing things will perish, including the flowers of light on the tree, which shall itself be uprooted and cast down through a hole in the sky around which he and his wife will be sitting, dangling their feet over the edge. A later scene finds the chief and his friends sitting around the tree. Compelled by custom to live out the dream lest the anxiety that it produced possess him, he suddenly seizes the tree and hurls it down, pushing his wife right behind it.

In the scene change the narrow focus of the hearer's imagination opens suddenly upon a vast sea of undulating waves, shrouded in a pearly auroral light that defines no horizon. Over the stillness on the sea moves a ripple of wind, the shadows of darting birds, until the mind's eye rushes in from the margins of eternity to focus upon the birds, wheeling and gathering over the sea, sensing in the rush of wind the fall from the sky. Then on their clustered backs they carry the woman cast down from the heavens and lower her gently onto the back of a great turtle floating upon the ocean. Beaver, Otter, and others are sent to gather mud from which a world can be made for her, but each fails in turn save Muskrat, who, sacrificing his life to the unlit depths of the sea, floats to the surface clutching a bit of mud in his mouth and paws. In some mysterious manner the value of his sacrifice and his fight is multiplied, and beneath the sleeping woman the earth spreads out borne on the carapace of the Great Turtle. And when the woman awakes from her swoon, time begins.

The Woman Who Fell from the Sky gives birth to a daughter who grows quickly and is herself magically impregnated, either by Turtle or Wind. During the gestation she hears two voices arguing inside her. The quarrel erupts into history when the Twins are born, normally in the case of Sprout, Good-Minded, or Sapling as he is variously called, but abnormally in the case of Flint or Evil-Minded, who bursts from his mother's armpit, killing her. Various parts of her body provide the first examples of edible plants in the Huron version. The Rival Twins engage in a dualistic struggle to establish the world, Flint creating exaggerations that threaten man's future and Sprout cutting them down to size. Sprout also releases the game animals that Flint has impounded. Throughout their contest the influence of the two women is heavily felt, Sprout being assisted by his mother and opposed by the Woman Who Fell from the Sky, who aids Flint. The world order is finally established, first when Sprout defeats Flint in a gambling contest establishing the seasons and second when Sprout defeats Flint in combat. After marrying a woman named Hanging Flower and establishing the family from which the contemporary Iroquois are descended, Sprout follows the Milky Way to join his defeated brother in the Skyworld. Among many non-Iroquoian peoples this Twins sequel holds a position independent of and more prominent than the Earth-Diver story and is closely related to the Star Husband tale.[11] Nevertheless, the activities of its hero, like those of Sprout, suggest that he, too, is clearly perceived as a transformer and culture hero.

The Algonkian peoples, among whom the Earth-Diver story has its widest circulation, tell it very differently, especially in the western Great Lakes area, where the Midéwiwin has influenced the story. Like the Iroquois, the Algonkians also begin with a protoworld populated by demiurges. According to the Menomini, for instance, the flood results from the desire of Manabozho the Trickster/Culture Hero to revenge the death of his brother, Wolf, at the hands of the underground supernatural beings.[12] In the middle of a lacrosse game that these spirits are watching, Manabozho drops his animal mask as Hare, assumes human form, and wounds them fatally with his arrows. Their death plunge into the Great Lakes sends waves of water to inundate the land. As the water rises, Manabozho takes to a tree, always just keeping ahead of the flood, which subsides just as he is running out of tree. Stranded above the flood, he calls to diving animals who all fail to bring up the necessary mud until Muskrat succeeds, and the world is created anew.

Unlike some other genres of oral literature, a creation myth such as the Earth-Diver story is not usually esoteric material, though it can become so when integrated with the origin stories of clans or religious organizations. In general, however, no restrictions are placed on the circumstances of its telling, precisely because it dramatizes in symbolic form the metaphysical principles by which the most profound mysteries of the community's daily experience are made intelligible. These principles of interpretation are displayed in the myth's prototypical events, which establish normative behaviors and relationships. For the myth's auditors in a community of belief, these serve as a guide for understanding and directing contemporary experience. In this manner the myth becomes, in Clifford Geertz's terms, both a "model of" the world and a "model for" the world, reflecting both metaphysical and ethical principles.[13]

William Fenton, the prominent Iroquoianist, has adopted a similar approach for interpreting the Iroquois Earth-Diver story. Among its prominent themes:

The earth is our mother, living and continually generating life.

Life is regular, cyclical, patterned by twos and fours, and these metaphysical patterns are models for ethical ones.

The world and all that is in it are endowed with Orenda (Power).

It is women who count (the Iroquois are matrilineal); paternity is secondary.

Restraint is important.

Thanksgiving and greeting maintain harmony in a hierarchical system by affirming right relationships.

Dreams compel their own fulfillment.

Finally, according to Fenton, the myth affirms that "culture is an affair of the mind."[14]

Among the essential principles articulated by any cosmological myth are the shape of the universe and the relationship between space and time. Clearly and consistently, in Indian myths three cosmic zones—the Skyworld, the Earth-Surface World, and the Underworld—are imaged. The passage of the mediational figure through these worlds creates different epochs, suggesting that time and space are mutually convertible, that to say "long ago" is the same as saying "far away." A corollary of this axiomatic, three-zone division is that passage between zones occurs along a definite path, an *axis mundi,* which may be imaged as the Milky Way, a sacred mountain, or a cosmic tree, and that passage can be taken in both directions. Finally, through a variety of images of transformation, the passage as fall illustrates the communication of sacred power into this world, where its effects are still visible. The act of communication establishes for all time the prototypical channel of power and provides, therefore, the means of access for all mankind to that power. Together with marvelous births, inner voices, Sky Parents, and a protoworld, these motifs link the Earth-Diver myth intimately with circumpolar, boreal shamanism, the origins of which, as indicated by the bear cult and cave paintings of man-animal transformations, lie deep in the Paleolithic past.[15]

Besides shamanism, another cultural institution frequently accounted for in the Earth-Diver myths is the origin of agriculture. Heavy dependence upon the corn-squash-beans complex seems to have come late for peoples like the Osage and the Iroquois, perhaps around A.D. 1000, although they had obtained these foods in small quantities through trade and scattered planting and had always gathered undomesticated plants.[16] Both myths contain startling flesh-to-plant transformations, which, despite their folkloric conventionality, nevertheless suggest the impact of an agricultural revolution upon a predominantly hunting culture. In the Iroquoian myth, this transformation is validated by the resolution in favor of the former pole, in the dualism of Sprout and Flint, Growth and Death, Peace and War, Corn and Meat. In the Osage myth the Elk joyfully gives itself up to the soil, producing from its hair all forms of vegetation, wild plants as well as cultigens.

The Earth-Diver is the story of the Fortunate Fall played out against a landscape more vast than Eden and yet on a personal scale equally as intimate. It is a story of losses, the loss of celestial status, the loss of life in the depths of the sea. But it is also the story of gifts, especially the gift of power over life, the gift of agriculture to sustain life, and the gift of the vision to understand man's place as somewhere between the abyss and the stars.

The Emergence Myth Complex

For the desert peoples of the Southwest and for other Native Americans, man did not fall out of the heavens to return there after his death, but issued instead from the womb of the Earth Mother and returned deep within her when his life was done.

Emergence myths are distributed over a wide area of Native America, excepting only the Northeast and the Northwest, but the story reaches its fullest development in the Southwest. Wheeler-Voegelin has established a high correlation between migration myths, some very extensive, and the Emergence myth itself, whose major motifs she summarizes: "Following ascent by natural or artificial means, the people and/or supernaturals (all living things) come from a hole in the ground after preparation of the earth for their habitation (or a scout's discovery of it as inhabitable.) The hole is thought to be preexisting or to be a cave or to have been bored by an animal, a series of animals or the culture hero(es). The means of ascent is either a vine, a stripling plant, a tree or mountain, or a combination of two or more of these. The emergence is actuated by the coming or subsidence of a flood (the termination of some other catastrophe)—in which case the emerging people are refugees—or by the desire for a place lighter, larger and better provided with subsistence forms than the underground habitation."[17] This core may be elaborated with preludes or sequels, so that a single performance may, as Bahr has reported for the Pima, last up to twenty-four hours.[18] All of these elements reach their maximum elaboration in the myths of the western pueblos of Hopi and Zuni, and in the origin myth of the Navajo.[19]

The Navajo came to the Southwest, most anthropologists believe, around A.D. 1500 from the Canadian Yukon, Athabascan peoples who knew nothing of agriculture or the Emergence myth. Under the pressure of forced association with Pueblo refugees from the Spanish reconquest following the Pueblo Revolt of 1680, they became agriculturalists and adapted the Pueblo Emergence story to their own purposes, later refining it through contact with the Hopi and the Zuni. For these borrowings they unabashedly give credit in their origin myth, acknowledging that when they emerged they met the Kisani, "house dwellers" or Puebloans, who were already living there, a people with hair cut straight across their brows who taught them about agriculture.

Navajo history began in the darkest, innermost womb of the Earth with several supernatural beings called Holy People, led by First Man and First Woman. Because they could not get along with the insect inhabitants of that world, they left it to emerge into the second, yellow world populated by small animals. This too they were compelled to leave, so they emerged into a third world, where First Man opened his medicine bundle and set out the prototypes of the present creation's mountains, rivers, plants, stars, and so on. With First Woman he also created the first human man and woman, the first Navajos, from two perfect ears of corn and eagle feathers. The people multiplied and grew factious over sexual jealousies and the adulterous behavior of the women, so that the men finally decided to abandon them. When monstrosities resulted from the perverse consequences of this separation, the men decided to firmly reestablish the social order. But Coyote stole Water Monster's baby, precipitating a flood that drove the people up a hollow reed into the fourth world. After the deluge had receded, First Man took out his medicine bundle, into which he had hastily gathered up the inner forms of creation he had made in the third world, and established this present world.

But the world was unstable. Through the scandalous behavior of the women in the third world, monsters roamed the earth and obstacles impeded travel over the land. The Great-Fear-Who-Walks-Alone, Those-

Who-Slay-with-Their-Eyes, He-Who-Kicks-Off-Cliffs, Shifting Sand
Dunes, all embodied man's deepest fear: that at bottom he and the world
through which he moved were finally unknowable and hence unmanagea-
ble. To change this the Holy People sent Changing Woman into the world
as an infant miraculously discovered one day by First Man and First Woman. She grew quickly to womanhood and gave birth to Twins fathered by
the Sun and his alter, the Moon. These two, Monster-Slayer and Born-for-
Water, set out to discover their paternity; after they pass the Sun's test, he
reveals his identity to them and arms them with powerful weapons they
use to slay the monsters and transform the face of the earth. Each then
embarks on a series of quests for ritual knowledge, which they bequeath to
the Navajo people in the numerous chantway myths of healing. In this
way the whole corpus of myths provides a dramatic inventory of Navajo
values.

The Zuni myth begins with the emanation of the Sky or Sun Father and
Earth Mother from the mind of Awonawilona, the asexual creator who
comes to be identified with the Sun emanation. Through the sky the Sun
Father passes on his daily journey lonely for companionship and care, for
people who will pray to him. To remedy this, he sends his two sons deep
within the fourth womb of the earth, where they find a world of total
darkness populated by groping amphibianlike creatures with slimy bodies,
horns, webbed feet, and tails, who live on wild grass and cannot even
control their bowels. It is chaos imagined as the antithesis of all they would
become. Under the leadership of the Twins, different birds are sent out to
the edge of the world to find a way out, but each in its turn fails. The
locust, however, is successful, and the people begin climbing out on a pine
tree cut for that purpose. Each time in a different direction, by means of a
different kind of tree, the people are led up through three more worlds
until they emerge into the light of their Sun Father. During their ascent,
the Zuni had constant rainfall, and may even have escaped through a cav-
ern with water rising just behind them. Many of their people had to be left
behind during their long stays in each world.

When they came out into the sun, they became aware of their deformi-
ties and did not know what to do. To guide them in this world, Spider
Woman chose an old man from the Dogwood Clan who was mysteriously
living just a short distance from the Emergence Rim. To him she gave
power to distinguish between the sacred medicine bundles and to fix the
ritual calendar, establishing him as the first sun priest and principal link
between the Zuni and the world of the supernaturals. It was he who led

the "Raw People," as they refer to themselves, to perfection at Zuni, the Center of the World.

The Transformation Era, which the Iroquois account for with the Rival Twins and the Navajo with the Hero Twins, the Zunis explain primarily by a migration sequel that details the events by which the "raw" people establish a social order. Fetishes and shrines are set apart, rituals are instituted, and religious prerogatives validated. Moieties of summer and winter people are established and clans formed. Numerous sacred societies, including the Kachina, Koyemshi, Newekwe, and Shomatowe, are denominated, each with its own developed mythology that branches from the main trunk of the origin myth at the appropriate point. Monsters are overcome by Twins analogous to the Navajo pair, and the shape of the world is stabilized by finding the Center and by a contest to determine the length of the day and the seasons. Agriculture is established, not only as a matter of economy but as the central metaphor for change. In short, having achieved the Center of the world, the Zuni have become their present selves.

The Zuni myth, and to a lesser extent the Navajo myth as well, demonstrate a high degree of what Laura Thompson in speaking of the Hopi has called "logico-aesthetic integration."[20] Though these peoples recognize categories of things based on physical differences that approximate Western scientific notions of phylum, order, and species, "they also have a system of cross-classification not recognized by Western science, which cuts across the empirically established, mutually exclusive orders, and closely relates phenomena from different classes or species into higher orders, which function as independent wholes in the cosmic scheme."[21] One of the purposes of the Emergence myth is to display dramatically this "system of interdependent relationships which give basic structure to the universe,"[22] by correlating, through a network of symbolic association, any number of elements, including kinship, sex, animal, bird, and plant species, minerals, colors, directions, seasons and other meteorologic phenomena, topographic features, and supernatural beings. This intersection of the physical and metaphysical, of which the Center is the prime symbol, provides a place, function, and significance for all elements of creation in a highly integrated system emphasizing what the Navajos call *hózhó* or "beauty," a concept of wholeness, balance, and integrity of form or being, closely related to the Greek *harmonia* or the Hebrew *shalom*. The value of such a system is clear. In a world so structured and charged with the power to affect human life dramatically, it is important to know, for instance, that medical problems have a metaphysical as well as a physical cause, and to seek out not only a physician but a medicine man.

Perfectionism marks the history of emergent peoples. Sometimes this impetus to perfection is expressed through an additive principle, by means of which new life forms are added in each successive world toward the final, total inventory. These man recognizes, names, and appropriates into his logico-aesthetic system, so that by the time the people emerge, the inventory of original inner forms has been completed, although they may later be transformed in their outer appearance. But progress also occurs on clearly evolutionary lines that illustrate changes in physical form, habitation, food, and behavior. Sometimes, as in the Pima-Papago myth, change is expressed as a series of destructions and re-creations, and a race or races of protomen precede the first appearance of real humans, a distinctly Mesoamerican touch. The Navajos, for instance, imagine an emerging race of insectlike people, later supplanted by the uniquely created parents of the Navajo. The Zuni, however, see themselves remaining as persistent identities throughout. Rather than being the last in a series of creations, they undergo a process of continual change from slimy, amphibian creatures of uncertain form, "raw" people, into a human form that is fixed or "cooked" after emerging into the daylight of the Sun Father. This humanization process is further characterized in the Zuni and Hopi myths by a shift in eating habits and residential patterns from wandering, wild seed-grass eaters to city-dwelling agriculturalists.

This processual dynamic of the Emergence myth admirably fits it to a number of ritual functions, especially in view of the fact that man's progress through the lower worlds comprehended moral as well as a physical evolution. Adultery and other forms of sexual and social irresponsibility, which violated the normative categories of relationship, were the source of the violence and discord that drove the protomen from the lower worlds in the Hopi and Navajo stories. In this the Hopi and Navajo differ from the Keresans and the Zuni, for whom the Emergence was an act of good will on the part of the Creator, who leads his people to him either personally or through agents. In both cases, man is remade, becomes perfected, and this establishes the myth's power as a metaphor for integration of all kinds. Since the disruption of the "logico-aesthetic" order of the world is at the root of all mental and physical illness, social disruption, agricultural failure, natural disasters, and other historical events, one must return through ritual, either individually or communally, to the place and time of Emergence, when the earth was young and men were "raw," and there begin anew the process of reforming self, society, or cosmos according to the prototypical pattern.

Like the Earth-Diver story, the Emergence myth and its migration sequel establish certain principles clearly. Some of the following principles and their corollaries have been stated explicitly for the Navajo by Clyde Kluckhohn.[23]

The world is a cyclically ordered, living reality of fragile relationships among intelligent, volitional beings, to whom man is intimately related through his prior forms and history.

All things are complementary. Nothing is whole or sufficient in itself. Mind, body, spirit are interrelated.

Man's role is actively to maintain harmony and integration among the elements of creation through ritual.

Control, order, is good; lack of control, disorder, is not.

The world is dangerous because nature is more powerful than man, but is not necessarily feared because power is available for all contingencies.

"Sin" and illness are disorder; disorder does not accrue guilt; it requires only repair.

Like produces like, and the part stands for the whole. This is the best of all possible worlds; it is this life that counts.

Nothing is ever lost; there is an economy even in dying.

In this light the Emergence myth and its sequels encode in dramatic form the metaphysical principles by which man comes to understand the significance of his presence in the world, contemplating the print of his foot in the damp earth of the Emergence Rim, upon which he first stood in the light of the sun.

The Trickster

The nature of the character conveniently called the Trickster is in fact an elusive one. The ambiguity inherent in his nature and the source of his power are a mystery to his creators and creditors. Dorsey and Kroeber identify the Arapaho "Nihansan" clearly as both a Trickster and a Transformer. Lowie finds the Crow Indian figure to be similarly ambiguous, writing that "Old-Man-Coyote not only figures at different times as transformer, trickster and founder of customs, but changes his character even in the same part of the cycle. At one time he assumes towards Cirape the part of a benevolent physician, at another he is humiliated by his friend's superior powers thwarting an attempted theft, again he is the trickster duped by his companion's luck or cunning."[24] One persona, the sum of all possibilities, can encompass at least three distinct roles: the aggressive Culture Hero like Monster-Slayer, the cunning Promethean Culture Hero, and the bumbling, overreaching Trickster.

His behavior is always scandalous. His actions were openly acknowledged as madness by the elders who performed the stories with obvious relish on many winter evenings. Yet these same respected voices would solemnly assert the sacredness of these very tales, which always involved the most cavalier treatment of conventionally unassailable material like sexuality or religion. To many Westerners reading these stories for the first time, it seemed at best a puzzling inconsistency and at worst a barbaric mystery that in many tribal mythologies this idiot and miscreant was in some unaccountable way also the culture hero.

The trickster figure is variously personified in a number of regional cultural traditions: in the Far West as Coyote, in the Northwest and Arctic as Raven, in the East as Hare, in the North Woods as Canada Jay or Wolverine, on the Plains as Spider or Old Man. Tricksters are well known under these guises; few have a generic name, like the Winnebago's Wadjunkaga or "tricky one," that does not imply an animal form. Yet despite their tail, paws, muzzle, or beak, and inevitably, odor, they are properly spoken of as personified, for they are imagined as behaving like humans in thought as well as deed, and their outward appearance is predominantly anthropomorphic. They can exchange their animal and human forms at will, and frequently do so to evade or deceive others, but their motivations are recognizably human.

The tales, too, are protean. Sometimes a story is told anecdotally, a compression of traditional humor and wisdom that derives its power from its pointed applicability to the situation motivating its telling. At other times it can be elaborated with the addition of great detail, the multiplication of incidents, and extensive dialogue. Most collections of trickster stories gathered by anthropologists before 1940, however, are impoverished performances, the result of poor elicitation methods and hand-recording. The real art of such storytelling is only visible when stories are performed in appropriate situations.[25]

Some Trickster stories, especially those focusing on bodily function, undermine man's belief in his own ability to govern himself.[26] Typical of these are stories surrounding the Winnebago Trickster's ropelike penis, which he keeps in a box he carries with him (as if he had it under complete control) but removes only too readily, commanding it to slither across a lake and have intercourse with the chief's daughter bathing near the far shore. Most of these tales, including those focused on food like the Laxative Bulb or the Reflected Fruit, are in the best burlesque tradition and provide a telling commentary on the great lengths to which men will go to satisfy an enormous desire to which they surrender themselves and yet over which they pretend to maintain absolute control.

A second type of story uses these bawdy elements to heighten a satire on social or religious customs. A widespread story known to folklorists as the Duped Dancers speaks to the hazards of blind faith, the inordinate curiosity about sacred things, and the naked vanity apparent when power is desired for its own sake. Hungry as usual, Trickster encounters a group of animals or ducks who appear to him as a possible lunch. He deceives them with the offer of sacred songs into dancing with their eyes shut, at which moment he slays them. Unfortunately he falls sleep as the ducks are roasting and wakes to find that his anus has failed to guard the meal as he directed and all has been lost to a hungry fox. In the tale's fullness, comic if not poetic justice is well served, for the Trickster and Tricked have both been shown to be victims of their appetites, and the noblest institutions of man susceptible to being converted into the meanest, although not without great cost to all. Nevertheless, the very suggestion in a community of belief that ritual may have its origins in such self-delusion is dangerous to contemplate.

A third type of tale, one in which Trickster appears in human form, is an undisguised attack on the dangers of institutional power in a social setting. Typical of these are stories of Trickster's "bad" behavior at clearly identifiable tribal rituals, such as the Winnebago story of Trickster at the Warbundle ceremony. Another widespread story, Trickster Marries the Chief's Son, illustrates the danger of confusing the power of the office with the power of man. What is so horrific about the story is that the chief has behaved in an unthinkably dangerous, foolish, and autocratic way. He has pledged his son's hand and the tribe's future to a woman who is an absolute stranger, without kin of any kind in the village. He has accepted her on the recognizance of an old woman, whose stereotyped position in Winnebago literature as a marginal figure living at the end of the village should signal distrust, especially when she assumes the role of town crier, normally reserved for people of high standing. That the chief should encourage his daughters to address the disguised Trickster as "sister-in-law" suggests that for him the personal satisfaction of his son's marrying what appears to be an attractive woman is more important than his responsibility to con-

clude a sound marriage for the sake of the tribe. The shock of recognition
that accompanies the disclosure that the "bride" is Trickster is a measure of
the ease with which people in the most responsible positions can pridefully
delude themselves and precipitate their own downfall.

The effectiveness of Trickster in undermining social order makes him
the appropriate vehicle for attacking the pomposity and revealing the ulterior motives of invading peoples as well. The Plains Cree tell a marvelous
story of how Wisahketchak the Trickster went furtrapping.[27] After mixing
up some poison and fat into little cakes, he gathered all the furbearing
animals together and began to preach to them and concluded his remarks
by offering them this "communion." With their skins he settled his debts
at the post. The tale is a stinging attack on the perceived relation between
Catholic priests and the French fur trade, historically documented as a
matter of policy, which bound a man's body and the labors of this life to a
credit system at the trading post and the efforts of his spiritual life to a
postponed reward beyond the grave. Native Americans also adapted many
European tales like the Money Tree or Excrement Gold, in which the native Trickster pokes fun at the white man's avarice or stupidity by taking
advantage of his preoccupation with power and self-importance.

In *The Trickster* (1956), from which many of the preceding examples are
drawn, Paul Radin advanced a Jungian interpretation of the Trickster as an
image of man's psychic evolution "from an undefined being to one with
the physiognomy of man, from a being psychically underdeveloped and
prey to his instincts, to an individual who is at least conscious of what he
does and who attempts to become socialized."[28] But anthropologists question what some psychologists take for granted; it is not at all clear, although terms like "cultural patterns" might seem to suggest it, that there
is anything like a collective community psyche that might generate what
Jung calls a "collective representation." And insofar as all psychoanalytic
systems reflect Euro-American cultural patterns, their usefulness outside
those spheres is even more limited than within the domain of their origin.

A second area of difficulty with this psychological interpretation is
structural and folkloristic; insofar as it represents long-term changes, character development of this type requires an ordered sequence of events in
coherent narrative. Cycles of Trickster tales cannot be random aggregations
of stories linked only by a picaresque protagonist, but must show an integration of plot and theme over an entire sequence of tales. More likely than
not, however, the patterning of the Winnebago cycle is not an inherent
feature, but the consequence of a long historical association with neighbor-
ing Algonkian peoples, whose Trickster cycles conclude with culture-hero

episodes as a result of the later accretion of origin myth material from the Midéwiwin society. Most Trickster tales are not told as elaborate cycles, but emerge singly, where circumstances provoke their telling for didactic purposes, or a few at a time in the evening. In neither case does the function seem to be to display the image of an evolving psyche, for the brevity of the tales and the fact they are told singly or in pairs preclude the narrative expanse needed to show great change. Rather an enduring, polyvalent symbol is unveiled, one that holds all meanings in suspension without development, climax, or the ultimate resolution of ambiguity.

Both Radin and Franz Boaz were rightly criticized by M. L. Ricketts for their attempts to separate Trickster cycles into tales of deception, which they had judged to be original to the figure's characterization, and tales of transformation and explanation, which they had judged to be intrusive. Tales like the Theft of Fire, which feature a cunning Trickster/Transformer who uses deception to acquire a fit gift for mankind at the cost of some bodily transformation, support Ricketts's claim that "the Trickster-transformer-culture hero is in origin a unitary figure, despite his complexity."[29] And through his choice of example tale, Ricketts hints darkly at what he considers the Trickster's most vital function: parodying shamanic practices like human-animal transformations, consulting spirit advisers, leaving the body for soul-flights to other worlds, and so on. The recognition of structural similarities between narrative and ritual, plot and action, point to a mutually affirmed world view assessed from different perspectives. But the difference is not, as Ricketts suggests, a matter of credibility—that ritual reverences what trickster tales parody—as much as it is the loss of vitality that comes when belief is institutionalized in normative cultural practices. It is not the religious conception of the world but its unquestioning acceptance that Trickster undermines.

In the course of their daily lives, most people, regardless of the culture in which they live, never question the cultural symbols embodying the principles by which they make sense of their experience. Living entirely "within" them, so to speak, they take them for granted until the experience of something radically different challenges the validity of the model itself, as the Galilean controversy did for Catholic Europe or the pillaging of Tenochtitlán by the returned "culture hero," Quetzalcoatl/Cortez, did for the Aztecs. As useful for ordering experience as cultural categories are, however, the culture of which they are a part would ultimately fail if catastrophe were the sole means by which anything could be called into question. Here is the virtue of a fiction like Trickster and his stories. As a made thing, a fiction, both the character and the narrative in which he lives have their own sets of rules that proclaim their artificiality and hence their "unthreatening" nature. Outside the system of norms established by the myths of origin and transformation, he becomes a useful, institutionalized principle of disorder. As an "outsider," Trickster can suggest the dangerous possibility of novel relationships between form and function (The Bungling Host story), sex and role (Trickster Eats the Children), belief and practice (and of the religious satires like The Skull Trap or the Offended Rolling Stone), kin and clan (Trickster Marries the Chief's Son), even appetite and will (The Laxative Bulb, the Giant Penis). He provides, in Barbara Babcock's terms, the "tolerated margin of mess" necessary to explore alternatives to the present system, to contemplate change.[30] In response to questions from Barre Toelken, the Navajo storyteller Yellowman offered this explicit correlation between fiction and reality: "Why tell them [the stories] to adults? 'Through the stories everything is made possible.' Why did Coyote do all those things, foolish on one occasion, good on another, terrible on another? 'If he didn't do all those things, then those things would not be possible in the world.' "[31] In his flauntings and his failures, Trickster offers us through his inversion of norms a reflex image of what is probable, preferred, or absolute, and a direct image of what is possible.

This ambiguity inheres in the storytelling dynamic itself. The tales first mobilize the audience's inclination to alter or abolish the system or categorical restraints by developing the story through the eyes of the Trickster figure, in whom, as Jung suggests, we recognize, however guiltily, some of ourselves. The tale then compels the audience to reaffirm those same beliefs that it has been momentarily permitted to question by manipulating it into laughing at the humiliation of the figure with whom it has so recently and so closely identified. Yet in this ambivalent situation, even laughter is suspect of more than one interpretation, as Bruce Grindal discovered collecting Trickster-figure tales among the African Sisala.[32] He observed that while adult storytellers valued the outcomes of the stories, laughing at the Trickster's humiliation which served them as a model for punishing contrariness, juvenile listeners responded more to the deceptions in the plot, ignoring the outcome and interpreting Trickster as a model for evading responsibilities derived from adult-sanctioned social categories. While it is commonly supposed that Trickster tales are told to illustrate the consequences of unacceptable behaviors, so that the affirming, concluding laugh, which liberates the audience while it condemns the Trickster, is the consequential one, Grindal's work with juvenile auditors suggests that the critical laughs are the intervening ones that sustain Trickster and implicate the audience in his madness.

By calling a particular category into question, the Trickster tale effectively establishes the much larger principle that all of culture, not just behaviors or institutions but the rules that govern them, is artifice. In this way, he deprives the distinction-making process of any ultimate and absolute necessity. From the perspective, then, of all those who have a great deal invested in the established social order, Grindal's Sisala elders, for instance, Trickster tales can be viewed as dangerous, corrupting. Among the Winnebago, Radin noted that members of the tribe trying to introduce the Peyote cult in the face of conservative opposition used Trickster in two ways. On the one hand they used him as a model for their own innovation—an "anticulture" hero, if you will—pointing especially to his satire of the traditional Warbundle Ceremony; on the other hand, they willingly used his characteristically superficial reading of situations, a trait that constantly gets him into trouble, as an image of the conservatives' opinionated foolishness.[33]

To the degree that man is never fully enculturated, the child and dreamer in each of us acknowledges that we are, as Clifford Geertz suggests, "unfinished animals."[34] Trickster is in the business of keeping us that way, of insuring that man remains "unfinished" by fossilized institutions, open and adaptable instead to changing contemporary realities. Trickster is the image of man continually creating himself, never finishing the task of distinguishing through encounter the Me from the not-Me, complementing the Culture Hero, whose function is to model the norm. Together the two save us, one from sterility and the other from anarchy. It is not true, as Ricketts would have us believe, that "he has 'gone away' and no longer has any direct influence in the world."[35] His name may have changed, his animal mask exchanged for another, but the Trickster is still around somewhere, just going along.

Chapter Two
Oratory and Oral Poetry

In the mountain mesa country of western New Mexico, beneath a darkly blazing star-filled sky, beneath the village, in the deeper, darker, sacred kiva-womb of the earth, while the world waits for the winter solstice and the rebirth of the sun, firecast shadows of masked figures move on the walls. Beneath the ladder of Emergence, which reaches through the ceiling entrance to the world of the Sun Father, the solemn voice of the Sayatasha priest announces the occasion:

> And now indeed it has come to pass
> When the sun who is our Father
> Had yet a little way to go to reach his left-hand altar,
> Our daylight father,
> Pekwin [sun priest] of the Dogwood clan,
> Desired the waters, the seeds
> Of his fathers,
> Priests of the masked gods . . .

The voice continues to roll like distant thunder telling how the priests would work through a night of cornmeal, pollen, stars, and prayersticks to bring life to the people through their chant.[1]

Far away, in the heart of the continent, Keokuk, the Sauk leader, addresses the peace commission attempting to resolve land disputes among the whites, the Sioux, and the Sauk: "You will now hear how my heart and the hearts of my chiefs and warriors, standing around me are placed."[2] In both instances, the word is not merely a linguistic sign, purely instrumental, a mere means of communication. It is announced, a breathing out of the life that is within, capable of providing a construction of reality that is unique to the speaker. For all of these reasons, the act of speaking, and not just the subject of the speaking, was considered to be charged with power, creative and not merely descriptive, sacred.

This seems especially true of oratory and poetry (chant or song), where the increasing formalization of the expression heightens the intensity and focuses the power of the communication. Donald Bahr observes that the

Pima and Papago have articulated a concept of "strength" that in its most basic form is simply a matter of utterance volume but may also be extended to include utterance rhythm.[3] "Secular" forms like oral history and other narrative, as well as homiletic preaching derived from the Christian tradition, are all communications entirely within the secular sphere—i.e., between men—and require little "strength." Intermediate forms like ritual oratory, however, are addressed both to the people present and to remote supernaturals and, in order to reach beyond the sphere of immediate attendants, are uttered with more "strength." Finally, ritual song is sung intensely with full "strength," since it is directed only to the supernaturals beyond. The movement from narrative to song suggests that rhythm as well as volume is also part of the definition of "strength." Gary Gossen observed a similar conceptualization among the Chamula Maya of southern Mexico, which they call "heat." As expression in Chamula becomes more formalized, "progressively more heat of the heart is required for good performance and verbal control because the speaker is under progressively more restraints of style, content, form and setting."[4] In general, then, oratory, song, and especially ritual poetry are the most highly wrought forms of verbal art.

Oratory

From the first centuries of white settlement in America, the oratorical ability of Native Americans, their artful talent for persuasion, was noted by Europeans. Perhaps the moment of highest praise came from Thomas Jefferson in his *Notes on the State of Virginia* (1784): "Of their eminence in oratory we have fewer examples, because it is chiefly displayed in their own councils. Some, however, we have, of a very superior lustre. I may challenge the whole orations of Demosthenes and Cicero, and of any more prominent orator, if Europe has furnished more eminent, to produce a single passage, superior to the speech of Logan, a Mingo chief, to Lord Dunsmore, then governor of this state."[5] But as Edna Sorber has pointed out, praise of native oratory was often uncritical, stemming from deeper motives.[6] Under pressure of European criticism attacking everything from the American climate to its flora and fauna, whites often asserted the abilities of Native Americans like Mingo in order to defuse such fears and heighten the value of America as a place of prospective settlement. If this is true, and it no doubt is in part, it is also true that early criticism of Indian oratory also stemmed from ulterior motives. It was often explicitly racist and based on the preconception that because Indians were "savages," they could produce nothing of worth, certainly nothing comparable to Demosthenes or Cicero. As a consequence of this debate, elements of imagery became fused, and the familiar noble savage became the "noble eloquent savage," and the ignoble savage, the ignoble, inarticulate Indian.

Of the forms of verbal art under discussion here, oratory occupies an intermediate position. It tends to be less discursive in form and more clearly marked by recurrent patterns of stylistic features than narrative, yet it never achieves the stylistic intensity and formality of ritual poetry. And despite appearances suggested by anthologized material, Native American oratory is not a single phenomenon. The limited range of content in the majority of Indian orations that have been preserved is very misleading. Records of speeches were kept by white men only as a habitual response to preserving in writing resolutions to military and political activities involving land. But Indian speeches, a few of which have been recorded by anthropologists, dealt with a wide field of subjects and occasions, including the dedication of a tipi or lodge, exhortation on the occasion of a burial, the recitation of war or hunting exploits, petitions and presentations to ranking officials, and a myriad of ceremonial activities.[7] As situated communication, then, distinctions in the field of oratory depend most importantly, as Bahr's observations among the Pima and Papago so well illustrate, on who is being addressed, by whom, and under what circumstances.

Ritual oratory occurs within the tribal community (the supernaturals of one community do not presume to address another community), either between the people and one of the representatives of the supernaturals, as in the Pima and Papago instance, or between the people and supernaturals who are not present, as in the Iroquois Longhouse speeches. Among the Iroquois, who have always valued fine speaking, occasions for eloquence occurred not only in council and treaty orations or in political speeches but in speeches for mourning dead chiefs and installing new ones in the Ritual of Condolence, in curing, and in the Handsome Lake religion and the Longhouse religion.[8]

The latter is exemplified by the Thanksgiving Address, which opens and closes every Longhouse ritual as an expression of gratitude directed to the hierarchically ordered powers of the cosmos. After a short prologue, the speaker addresses the assembly of those present. Then he turns his attention first to the terrestrial powers (Waters, Grasses, Fruits, Vegetables, Animals) and then to the cosmological forces in the Sky (Sun, Moon, Stars, Winds, Thunders). Finally his attention is turned to the powers who dwell beyond the inverted bowl of the sky, those who live in the world from which the Sky Woman fell (see Chapter 1, Earth-Diver). These include the Four Beings, powers who monitor the cosmos and human affairs; Handsome Lake the Prophet; and the Creator. By going "beyond the sky," the speech achieves both a literal height in space but also a depth in time, returning to the Creator and his preexisting world.[9] According to Michael Foster, the aesthetic of contemporary Iroquoian oratory values a speaker who can balance all these essential components in a highly structured narration of appropriate proportions and reasonable length, and one who has a good memory for exact order and full detail. In addition, the speaker should have a clear speaking voice capable of communicating feeling. He should also be adaptable, which means knowing not only the procedural rules for more than one longhouse, but also knowing more than one Iroquoian language. Finally, he should be discreet, self-effacing, and of sound judgment.[10]

Secular oratory is situated within a tribal (Hopi grievance chants) or intertribal setting (council speeches). The most extensive collection of secular orations are the recorded speeches associated with treaty-making and the westward expansion of the United States into Indian lands.[11] One of the most famous instances of such a speech was Red Cloud's 1870 address in New York's Cooper Union. Contrary to the popular understanding of communication in an oral culture, Red Cloud labored hard preparing this speech, for he clearly felt himself to be the official representative for thirty-nine bands of his fellow Sioux. When the moment came to deliver his speech, he began by rising from the floor upon which he had been seated and, in one motion, drawing his blanket around himself "majestically." Then he raised his arms up to the heavens, and bringing them slowly down, began to pray. During the speech, he used the pauses after each utterance necessary for translating the speech into English to survey his audience. After the address, which Horace Greeley's *Tribune* called a "remarkable triumph," the crowd was so reluctant to leave that it crowded around the Indians on stage, including Red Cloud, expressing their appreciation with such resounding applause and enthusiasm that officials encountered "considerable difficulty" getting not only from the stage to the door, but from the door to the hotel, and even from the hotel to the train.[12]

American Indians valued eloquence. Although the speeches when read can hardly approximate the impact of their first utterance, and although not all Indians spoke in the "classical" style of Demosthenes or Cicero, a few excelled in the role, and the records of their speeches preserve their art. In the end some, like Red Jacket, the renowned Seneca, rejected the title of warrior. "I am," he said, "an orator!"[13]

Lyric Poetry

Lyric poetry is song. Since the Renaissance the Western world has moved farther away from that concept of poetry, which was older than the Greeks, but it remains the distinguishing feature of lyric poetry in Native American oral traditions. Native lyric poetry differs from ritual poetry in several ways. First, unlike ritual poetry, the lyric is free from the context of a communal religious drama, although it may have religious connotations. Further, where ritual poetry is most frequently, although not exclusively chanted, lyric poetry is sung on melodic line, often with musical accompaniment. Most importantly, the lyric is intensely personal, shot through with highly connotative words that reflect the emotional response of the singer; it is seldom formulaic.

Almost all native songs were accompanied by percussive instruments, especially a variety of drums and rattles; occasionally these were augmented with flutes and, very rarely, stringed instruments. The primary melodic instrument was the human voice. Depending on traditional styles and the capacity of the language, the voice created a rhythmic melody in a number of ways. Music, rather than the words, seems to have been a more stable element in tradition lyric song.[14] Among the Eskimo, an entirely new set of lyrics may be adapted to a traditional melody, and the recurrence of the same rhythmic notations over a number of different Aztec poems suggests that this was also standard practice in cultures as remote and different as those in Mesoamerica. The traditional melodies testify to the venerable status of song and the continued identificaton of singing as a particularly human activity. The Maidu of California emphasize the fundamental role of song with a story about Coyote, their Trickster/Transformer, who gave the world songs, and "Robin-man [who] sang that which was pleasant to hear. He, they say, was the first created person—a man whose song passed across the valley, a man who found the world, a man who in the olden times sang very beautifully-sounding songs."[15]

The smaller portion of the lyric literature is composed of expressive lyrics that disclose the emotions of the speaker quite openly. In many instances they resemble in tone and subject matter, familiar Western types like the complaint, the ode, and the love song, although each tribe, of course, had their own aesthetic requirements and nomenclature for song types.[16] Consider the differences in the following two love lyrics. The first, by a singer from the Aleutian Islands of Alaska, expresses the almost tantalizing pleasure of rapt anticipation:

> I cannot bear it at all.
> I cannot bear to be where I usually am.
> She is yonder, she moves near me, she is dancing.
> I cannot bear it
> If I may not smell her breath, the fragrance of her.[17]

The speaker of this second poem, a Nootka woman, finds the perfect response to an annoying suitor who has convinced only himself of his attractiveness:

> Keep away.
> Just a little touch of you
> Is sufficient.[18]

Other expressive poems speak of the loss of innocence, of the joy at growing old and handsomely gray, of lost love, indeed, of the entire scope of emotional and social life.

Occasional lyrics are poetic responses to specific events. Many songs of leaving wife and home to go to war have been collected. Used-As-A-Shield sang a traditional theme in the face of death:

> The old men say,
> The earth only endures.
> You spoke truly.
> You are right.[19]

Songs of victory and the adventure of war have been taken into every literature in the world, although always accompanied by another kind of song, like this one sung by a young Sioux woman:

> As the young men go by,
> I was looking for him.
> It surprises me anew
> that he is gone.
> It is something
> to which I cannot
> be reconciled.[20]

This sense of loss often obscures any vague benefit that might accrue to a particular community through war, and this loss is borne expecially by

women, as one Papago woman sings what the men of her tribe do to their
traditional enemies, the Apache:

> Men shouting "Brother," men shouting "Brother"—
> Among the mountains they have taken little
>   Apache children
> Where the sun went down in sorrow.
> All women, what shall we do
> to realize this.[21]

Other kinds of occasional lyrics, each with their own more precise tribal
genre names and descriptions, include songs of praise, reporting the deeds
and extolling the names of particular individuals; elegies, more formal
expressions of grief than the wailing lament; and death songs, songs of
power sung in the face of imminent death.

Small and brief as these lyrics appear, intensity more than economy
seems to have been the major aim. Duration was savored through repeti-
tion, but length itself was not a value. Pleasure came from the artful use of
language, from word choice, the right turn of phrase, from novel imagery
and the relationship between music and words. Indeed, discovering the
right word, the word that fits, that makes things happen, that releases the
soul, lifting it up on a welling flood of song—finding that word was making poetry.

Eskimo lyrics supported this expressed concern for the shape and feel of
language, a crafting that starts with the gift of words following an intense
emotional experience. The Netsilik Eskimo poet Orpingalik reflected:

Songs are thoughts, sung out with the breath when people are moved by great
forces and ordinary speech no longer suffices. Man is moved just like the ice floe
sailing here and there out in the current. His thoughts are driven by a flowing
force when he feels joy, when he feels sorrow. Thoughts can wash over him like a
flood, making his blood come in gasps and his heart throb. Something like an
abatement in the weather will keep him thawed up, and then it will happen that
we, who always think we are small, will feel still smaller. And we will fear to use
words. But it will happen that the words we need will come of themselves. When
the words we want to use shoot up by themselves—we get a new song.[22]

But the gift of words is always jeopardized for the Eskimo by the necessity to fit them harmoniously to melody and rhythm, while dancing in the
center of the dancehouse, simultaneously drumming on a three-foot-di-
ameter single-skin drum and exhorting the chorus to respond, all in a per-

formance that could last for hours. The poem must be delivered fluently and perfectly under these conditions. The singer asserts: "I got my poem in perfect order. On the threshold of my tongue its arrangement was made."[23] When everything worked together, the song seemed to take a life of its own, to be born into the world through the throat of the singer, to reach out for others, and then to come back to him in the form of their chorus:

> My song, that one, it begins to want to come out.
> It begins to want to go out to my companions,
>   there being a request for singing,
>   there being a request for dancing.
> My song, that one, it only, it also comes back,
>   that one, my companions,
> Asking to be made happy.[24]

Only in performance was the life cycle of a song completed. For the Eskimo, song was a necessity, not an ornament, a way of making real and visible his relationship to the world. "My breath—this is what I call my song," Orpingalik said, "for it is just as necessary for me to sing as it is to breathe." In his language, in fact, the same word is used for both "song" and "breath."[25]

For the Aztec as well, lyric poetry was not a luxury but the result of an inner compulsion to articulate the space of man's life on earth. Poets and noblemen often gathered together to discuss the nature of art and poetry, a topic that led to more deeply metaphysical inquiries about life in a "world of continually perishing flowers." Thirty-six years before Cortez sacked Tenochtitlán (the present Mexico City), Tecayahuatzin, prince of Huexotzinco, called such a gathering to inquire into the nature of Truth and Art. One poet present, Ayocuan, expressed the dominant opinion of the day that all was vanity, the world but a place of fleeting moments. Cuauhtencosztli, another poet, doubted that anything, including art, had real life; all is illusion. Others responded by saying that poetry can help man to know the Giver of Life and can fill man with rejoicing. In the end the host, Tecayahuatzin, concluded that whatever value poetry may have for man's relationship to eternity, at least we can know through their poetry that "the hearts of our friends are true."[26]

Aztec poetry is filled with evocative imagery of birds, jewels, and especially flowers. The fragile beauty of the latter made them apt symbols not only for Art but for Life, as the Aztec envisioned them both. "Flower and song" was the Aztec term for poetry. Ayocuan, singing to his friends in the

garden, could evoke a number of associations at once with this flower
imagery:

> The exotic perfume of flowers filters down,
> Friendship, a rain of precious flowers,
> Plumes of white heron interlaced
> With the precious cut flowers.
> In the place of the branches,
> They go about sipping at the flowers,
> The lords and nobles.[27]

For all the beauty of their poetic language, the tone of Aztec poetry is
predominantly pathetic. For even at the moment of their ascendancy, no
people were ever more conscious of the transient nature of life, life as vibrant yet as frail as the flowers they so loved. Man lived, they believed, in
such a world, "a world of continually perishing flowers." On this earth
there was no truth save that of the fleeting moment. One poet wrote:

> Is it yet true there is living on earth?
> Not forever on earth; but a moment here.
> If it is jade it shatters,
> If it is gold it crumbles,
> If it is feather it rends.
> Not forever on earth; but a moment here.[28]

Death was inevitable and its radical order final. But for the poets, who
were all educated noblemen, change was not cataclysmic, except perhaps
at the end of the Great Year of fifty-two years. Rather it was a slow, subtle,
almost invisible, yet all-pervasive and sure, slipping toward the abyss of
forever.

This contemplation of death and change called forth two responses. The
first was to claim for Art, especially for poetry, an eternal character, a claim
founded on the belief that only those things that were invented or created
could ever reach the house of the golden bird, the House of the Sun, to live
there forever before the face of the Giver of Life. Art imitated the creative
activity of the Lord of Duality, for whom the whole universe was his dis-
guise or *nahaul,* and only in his perfect form was eternal life found. All else
would wither and pass away.

The second response to the transiency of life was to establish eternal
friendship through shared art. Flesh would certainly fall, but the spirit,
imbued with poetic vision and truth, would not fall. So among flowers

and song, the Aztec nobleman reached out not so much for eternal life as for "real living." The flesh was illusory, but in the spirit one might enter the house of the Giver of Life. For this present moment on earth, however, it was only in friendship created by sharing their lives in their poetry that men could ever "know each other's faces" and see the truth.

Ritual Poetry

The Aztec's longing for truth in a "world of continually perishing flowers" is only part of the larger native understanding that the power that maintains order and stability also actuates radical change. The immanent presence of this power, frequently incarnated in a variety of forms, was felt deeply. Sacred power was neither good nor evil, malevolent nor benificent, only awesome in its capacity both to create and to destroy, and wholly Other. In the face of such power, awesome yet coercible, ritual provided Native Americans a means to bring the apparently chaotic, disturbed, and accidental under control. To exercise this control over the power of the Sacred, Native Americans looked either to the priest or to the shaman or medicine man. Central to both shamanic and priestly religious traditions, however, was the power of the word, especially the sung or chanted word. As the Creator told the Iroquois, "Only the Word and also the Mind will be able to go on high."

Shamanism occurred throughout North America as the dominant mode of religious experience, except in the Southwest, where it was strongly overlaid by a neopriestly tradition of Mesoamerican origin. Solitude and physical ordeals induced visions and brought the shaman to an experience of near-death and resuscitation, which transformed him. To be a shaman or medicine man, in the words of the Caribou Eskimo shaman Igjugarjuk, is to "choose suffering," for only "solitude and suffering open the human mind."[29] The last things a shaman learned were songs and sacred words, usually given to him in the initiatory trance into which he had been cast by the visitation of his guardian spirit. Morris Opler discerned that a special relationship exists between "the Mescalero [Apache] and the power he 'knows,' 'to which he sings,' and 'which works through him,' as the phrases go. The songs or prayers of the ceremony he has learned, for instance, attract the attention of the power source and make it sensitive to his needs and requests."[30]

Shamanic songs tend to be short and dithyrambic, repeated over and over again to time kept by a rattle or a drum. Because shamanic poetry seeks to re-create a state rather than an event, it seldom develops lengthy

poems with a coherent narrative line recounting prototypical events from
the mythic past. Shamanic ritual achieves substantiality and duration in
time and space by repeating many different short songs in sequence, each
of which may be sung over and over again many times. This is the case for
the major rituals of the shamanic tradition in Native America, including
the Midéwiwin of the Chippewa, the Sun Dance of the Plains tribes, and
the later Ghost Dance. It is even true of the neopriestly ceremonies of the
Navajo medicine men. A compulsive tone pervades most shamanistic ritual poetry because the shaman believes that the faithfully uttered word
makes things happen. As in many dream songs, which are personal instances of shamanic song, confidence in the power of the Sacred incarnated
in the word can generate a triumphal tone.

Unlike shamans, whose knowledge of the supernatural was primarily
experiential, the priest acquired control over the sacred mostly through
formal training that molded his knowledge and practice to the orthodoxy
held by the class of priests to which he belonged. The Zuni, for instance,
have an office for someone who guards sacred chants, insuring their accuracy in transmission, and Navajo medicine men must involve themselves
in a lengthy apprenticeship given over mostly to the learning of songs.[31]
Religious poetry from a priestly tradition is usually very formal in tone,
befitting the dignity of the relationships enjoined upon both the human
and supernatural parties in the mythic past. Myth provides the narrative
line and context of meaning in the chant, for the priest, unlike the shaman, seeks to re-create a prototypical event. Also priestly religious poetry,
much more than shamanic poetry, is filled with references, often mythol-
ogically disguised, that provide actual instructions for performing the ritual. Priestly ritual poetry, especially the long chants from the Puebloan
Southwest, is distinguished from shamanic ritual poetry in two further
ways. First is the use of the implicitly metaphorical formula or stereotyped
expression, which binds the mythic prototype to the present event through
a fixed syntactic structure. The second is the use of elaborate systems of
typology and numerological, geographical, and chromological symbols
through which the present patient and rite are identified with the mythic
prototype.

Defining kinds of ritual poetry by external formal criteria is impossible
because these differ from culture to culture. Instead cross-cultural comparison of types of ritual poetry can be facilitated by examining the inner form
of the songs, and, because these depend on the context of ritual practice
and belief for their meaning, the nature of the event itself must be taken

into consideration. The two essential factors appear to be the human focus of the ritual, whether an individual or corporate identity (clan, secret society, religious fraternity, or tribe), and the conceptualized locus of supernatural power, whether in the mythic past or the eschatological future. Those rituals referring to the protypical past as their model are here denominated as Integrative, if they have an individual as their subject, and Restorative, if they take a corporate identity as their subject. Teleological rituals, which seek power from some end-time model, are either Redemptive, if the change they seek is within the individual, or Transformative, if they seek to change the social order.

Integrative ritual poetry. At no other time is man in such immediate danger as when he is undergoing radical change in his person. Although birth, the onset of puberty, sickness, and death are all transitory states, for their duration they effectively alienate man from the equilibrium of his former, harmonious state of being. Consequently, these dangerous moments in life are generally shrouded in rites of passage. [32] The primary purpose of these life-crisis rituals is to control the transition from one state to the next, and so effectively reintegrate the individual into the social and spiritual orders from which he has been temporarily alienated. This is accomplished by reestablishing his identity and experience as part of the pattern of prototypical events that established for all times the model by which the alienating effects of any life crisis can be nullified.

Birth was usually marked by a presentation ceremony or a later naming ceremony, the first of many the child would receive. These rituals were meant to identify the child as a unique and valuable member of the community, and to establish for him his initial relationships as a human being to the natural and supernatural orders. An Eskimo poem, sung by a shaman over a child born at Lyon Inlet on the Melville Peninsula above Hudson's Bay, compresses a life into a day, for the object of the song was to terminate the transition period as quickly as possible and hasten the child into the fullness of his new life:

> I rise up from rest,
> Moving swiftly as the raven's wing
> I rise up to meet the day—
> wa-wa.
> My face is turned from the dark of night
> My gaze toward the dawn,
> Toward the whitening dawn. [33]

In other cultures, including the Tewa and Omaha, songs were sung and prayers said to present the newborn child to the Sun or other powers in the universe. The Makah of Puget Sound sang songs projecting the child's future good fortune.[34]

Puberty rites occur widely throughout Native America and seem to have developed in many cases from a common protostructure. Girls' puberty rites, held at the time of the first menses, usually involved confinement for a ritual number of days (most often four) and the strict observance of certain taboos. Spiritual power was believed to accompany menstruation and women in this condition were forbidden from associating with hunters and warriors, perhaps because the effectiveness of these men as temporary agents of death would be nullified by the power of life represented by the woman's menses.

Puberty songs are of three types. Like many other ritual songs they may be simply *directional,* requiring in their texts that certain acts be performed. In the Combing Song of the Navajo *Kinaaldá,* the young girl is clothed in the beautiful garments of Changing Woman, each of which is named, and so identified with the Navajo image of beauty, fertility, and womanliness.[35] A second type of puberty song is *instructional,* since the puberty rite is often the vehicle for communicating to the new adult the esoteric knowledge associated with tribal mythology and ritual practice. A third type of puberty song is the *dawn song,* sung on the morning of the last day of the ritual. In these dawn songs, the young woman's entrance into adult life is celebrated while she runs toward the eastern horizon. These songs express the urgent desire to enter the new world of womanhood. The fact that many such ceremonies conclude at dawn affirms a link between the cosmic cycles and the changes bringing the young girls to womanhood. For this reason, many peoples understand puberty rites as touching upon the fate of the entire community as much as upon that of a single girl.[36]

Sickness and death also disrupt the harmony of one's relationships. Shamans believed that evil power incarnated in a foreign object lodged in the body was responsible for a patient's symptoms. In other cases, trespass on sacred space or other unsanctioned contact with the sacred could cause sickness. The remedy for the first was to remove the offending object, either by blowing an aspersion of medicinal plants upon it or by sucking it out. Sometimes the removal of the object was dramatically suggested, as in the Navajo Hoop (Tsepanse) Rite, in which the patient passed through four hoops, each of which, according to the sanctioning myth, further removed the skin of Coyote or Big Snake in which the patient was bound. In the case of pollution through contact with a sacred power, the patient is restored to normal order by journeying into the mythic past through the chant narrative, and there being identified with the culture hero who had acquired power for dealing with this disease by being himself the first victim. In the Navajo Windway the patient/hero is taken by Talking God through the four lower worlds in an Orpheus-like descent; at the end of his journey he confronts and defeats evil and then is brought back to the earth-surface world.[37] The several hundred highly repetitive and symbolic songs that typify the five- and nine-night healing ceremonies of the Navajo are the essential part of this healing ritual. Even in less developed ritual complexes, the shamanic sucking rites, for instance, the sleight-of-hand that produces the offending pebble from the shoulder, the medicines all are secondary. As one shaman told Ruth Underhill, "we could cure without that just by singing and remembering the [shaman's commissioning] vision. But the people need something to see."[38]

Death is always a traumatic experience for a community, but as a transition it was also understood to produce anxiety and other problems for individuals. If the dead was an enemy slain in battle, pollution contaminated the victor, who needed to be purified of the disposition that produced violence. In the Southwest contact with the enemy dead was complicated by the belief that all the dead resided in the clouds and brought rain; the taking of a life in an unsanctioned manner violated higher laws and could mean drought and starvation for the community. If the dead was a member of the community, much of the anxiety stemmed from the belief that the departed, now alone, would remain in the village, perhaps even take someone with him for companionship. This fear of the unseen power of the dead is commonly managed in native cultures by songs and prayers for the ritual expulsion of the dead. The Santo Domingo pueblo singer adopts the persona of the deceased to proclaim the departure of the beloved for the mythic place of emergence, *shipap*:

> All the white-cloud eagles,
> Lift me up with your wings and take me to *shipap*.
> And also you other eagles,
> Come and lift me up with your wings, 'way up high,
>   all over the world; no one can see the place
>   you are taking me.
> 'Way down in the southwest where our fathers and
>   mothers have gone,
> Put me there with your eagle wings.[39]

Through these ritual songs, Native Americans are able to restore harmony to personal lives disturbed by violent change and successfully reintegrate the individual into the social, natural, and supernatural orders from which he had been displaced.

Restorative ritual poetry.   Just as in moments of crisis the individual returns to the Past for new power, so also does the society of which he or she is a part. These rituals, often called world-renewal rituals, are prominent in agricultural societies but not restricted to them, as the Kwakiutl Winter Ceremonial and the Karok First Salmon Ceremony attest.[40] At moments of crisis, these rituals obtain power and order for the world by shaping contemporary reality to the mythical prototype, which transcends history.

The Zuni Shalako ceremony, a good example of this type of ritual, occurs just before the midwinter solstice to begin the Zuni ritual year.[41] At this time the kachinas or masked spirits, led by Pautiwa and his second, Sayatasha, come to the pueblo from their underground village to dance for rain and snow. Sayatasha's role is important. During the whole year, the individual who impersonates Sayatasha visits all the sacred springs around Zuni, reenacting the migration from the place of Emergence to the pueblo. He completes this task of commemoration and renewal by chanting a poem of over 750 lines during the course of an evening at Shalako and presenting the pueblo with a bundle of seeds to insure fertility in the coming year. This high purpose of renewing the world he expresses in images of plenty, announcing that he has come so that

> . . . their house may have a heart,
> That even in this doorway
> The shelled corn may be spilled before his door,
> That beans may be spilled before his door,
> (That the house may be full of) little boys
> And little girls,
> And men and women grown to maturity,
> That in his house
> Children may jostle one another in the doorway.

In this way life is renewed at Zuni.

Corn, sun, and water are the definition of existence at Zuni, and the process of symbolic association often links these phenomena in interesting ways. In Sayatasha's chant, for instance, the Zuni speak of themselves as the "daylight children" because of their emergence from the underground (see Emergence Myth). Light and breath are central metaphors for life. Life as duration and fulfillment is spoken of as a road of pollen, analogous to the path of cornmeal laid down by the priest from the base of the kiva's ladder to the altar, a metaphor that reveals the Zuni's dependence upon, even identification with, corn. Corn is often personified, but even when it is not, catalogs of "all the different kinds of corn" or references to prayer meal make corn a central element in Zuni poetry.

The most complex interrelationship of symbols at Zuni involves water. The primary focus of this interrelationship can be divided into springs or "standing water" and rain or "falling water." The symbolism of standing water is directly related to the myth of the origin of the kachinas: springs are entrances to the underwater home of the kachinas, and also recall that spring which emptied miraculously to provide a passage through which the Zunis emerged into this world. This last association is further extended by the metaphor in which the kiva is referred to as "the rain-filled room." Rain is distinguished as either "heavy" summer rain or the "fine" rain of spring showers. Clouds are the home of the ancestral dead, who are rain-makers, and also their "watery shields," which hide their faces from view. Clouds are also metaphorized in calling tobacco smoke "misty breath," invoking associations with the origin myth, wherein Awonawilona conceived of the universe and the clouds created by his thoughts condensed to form Sky and Earth.

Understanding the cultural references for these symbols, one begins to see clearly that they form a mimetic pattern the object of which is the insurance of fertility. By returning mythically to the time and place of creation, identifying the Sayatasha impersonator with the intentionality and power of the first being, Awonawilona, and in that context ritually duplicating the act of creation, Sayatasha and his party renew the world. The poem, then, speaks to us of man's need for both order and rebirth: without renewal and rebirth, the initially vitalized order of life sickens and dies; without harmony and order the generative dynamism of life leads to chaos and conflict. But although the poem begins with this dualism as a basic premise, the renewal that is at the heart of the Shalako ceremony mediates this dualism by insisting that the only way the power of life can be brought into the world is through a return to order. In the end Order and Generation are held in the necessary pose of creative tension only in the ritual language of the poem, which announces, "Let it be here . . . . Let it be now."

Redemptive ritual poetry. It is only the perspective of man's historical condition that makes a distinction between the mythic past and the eschatological future possible, since both coexist in the incomprehensible, a historical Now of the Center. But man's present exigencies provide him his only point of departure for any spiritual journey, in relation to which it may be safely, if metaphorically, said that man journeys backward beyond the past in Integrative and Restorative rituals and forward beyond the future in Redemptive and Transformative rituals.

Redemptive ritual is focused on individual change. The frequent use of first-person point of view in the poetry of these rituals illustrates this personal search for a new status, which David Aberle sees as the defining characteristic of Redemptive ritual.[42] Any accompanying rejection of elements of the present social order is secondary to this inner search, which features two constants: overcoming one's own resistance to change and changing one's relationship with the world. The former is frequently accomplished by penances and other self-inflicted mortifications aimed at destroying the old self, but often such resistance vanishes with little or no exertion at all. Changed relationships with the world are often made manifest by joining secret societies such as the Midé or the Plains dream societies, whose members have shared similar experiences or dreamed of the same totem animal.

Dream songs occur in every area of the native North America, although they are less prominent in the Arctic and the puebloan Southwest. The power of dreams to reshape identity about an interior vision revealed by the unconscious became the central religious experience of the Plains peoples, among whom dreams were badges of identity. Even where dreams did not serve this function, they were considered the source of wisdom and creativity. Dreams have two characteristics that are important to understanding the personal yet sacred experience rendered in the dream song. First, they are so clearly identified by the dreamer as his own that they become the distinguishing factor in the development of identity, as this song of a Clayoquot woman illustrates:

> Do not listen to the other singing.
> Do not be afraid to sing your own song.[43]

Nothing is more personal than one's dreams, which constitute a secret well of power from which one can draw strength and general spiritual renewal. Second, dreams communicate a sense of their implicit rightness to the dreamer. Frances Densmore recorded a Chippewa dream song in which the dreamer was only interested in expressing that radical faith or confidence that derived from his dream; it says simply, "The heavens go with me."[44] This radical faith reflects a sense of election not unlike the tone found in the song of an Eskimo woman, Uvavnuk, who felt she had absorbed the power of a falling star:

> The great sea
> Has sent me adrift,
> It moves me as the weed in a great river,
> Earth and the great weather
> Move me,
> Have carried me away
> And move my inward parts with joy.[45]

Almost invariably, dream songs focus on natural phenomena such as animals, birds, stars, the wind, any of which may become the individual's dream totem if the song is used as a badge of identity. Almost all dream songs are short; narration is minimal. Often time and place (or any form of setting) are avoided. The image, which functions as a mask of the soul in its interior dialogue, is the essential feature. A strange union of abstraction and concreteness, heightened by brevity and in many cases a repetitive form, gives dream songs such a surrealistic visionary quality that they attain a universal character despite their identification with a particular individual.

Several types of dream songs can be distinguished in terms of the relationship between the subject and the narrator. In the first type of dream song, the narrator recalls how he has been commissioned by a water spirit or manido, while a Sioux dreamer tells how a totem animal addressed him. A second type of dream song is indirectly narrated. The dreamer is not present in the song text to provide a familiar reference; only the image is given, almost hypnotically: "owls / hooting / in the passing night / owls / hooting."[46] In the third type of dream song the speaker repeats the words the totem animal spoke to him. A Sioux song, sung to the dreamer by an elk, alludes to the totem's strength, steadfastness, and nobility, while offering an ideal of character toward which the dreamer may strive. Still a fourth type of dream song explicitly indicates that something has been made sacred. When the Sioux speaks of the deer's being made sacred "for me," the deer becomes, in Emerson's words, an "exponent of meaning," the fundamental term of relationship to the world, which establishes this man's identity as distinct from others.

The individual may assert his newly changed status and identity by joining a secret society. The Plains dream societies, for instance, included only those who had dreamed of the group's animal totem; typical are the

Elk, Buffalo, and Horse dream societies Densmore noted among the Teton Sioux. Dream societies have their own group songs which reflect consciousness of the totemic animal and are characterized by the same brevity and singleness of image as individual dream songs. One Horse Society song, in which the group identity is made explicit, has the quality of a vision, its repetitive structure almost miming a stallion's prancing:

> see them
> prancing
> they come
> neighing
> they come
> A Horse Nation
> see them
> prancing
> they come
> neighing
> they come[47]

The Midéwiwin, the extensively developed Medicine Society of the Chippewa, is another secret organization; members are initiated into the society and in the course of their lives advance through several degrees in the Midé lodge. The words of the Midé songs, like those of the Walam Olum, a long Delaware narrative poem, were prompted from images painted on bark. Midé songs are characteristically brief, imagistic, and relate a single manifestation of a spirit (*manido*) or its power.

Another Redemptive ritual was the Sun Dance, a ceremony widely distributed across the Plains, which reached its maximum elaboration among the Arapaho, Cheyenne, and Sioux. While the Sun Dance often prompted creation of large numbers of songs—Clark Wissler records 413 for the Blackfeet ritual—the songs themselves, like others based on a shamanistic dream culture, were very brief.[48] Yet the redemptive nature of the historical ritual is clear in its structure.

The opening dance was followed by a ritual exchange of presents and an invocation. Then sacred "sun-gazing" dancing took place. Some men simply danced while gazing at the sun; others lacerated themselves during the dancing to demonstrate their courage and willingness to sacrifice; still others danced with the whole weight of their body suspended from the center pole on rawhide thongs skewered through their pectoral muscles. Occasionally the wife of a dancer might dance with him and sing a song of encouragement, for each man danced to fulfill a vow. At noon of the first or second day, the principal celebrant, called the Intercessor, would sing a song invoking the sun's trail, and another song identifying himself with the sun and the moon through his several totems. During torturous dancing, songs were sung expressing confidence that the sacred power, Wakan Tanka, would transform their lives with goodness and prosperity, courage and victory. When the entire ceremony was concluded, the Sun Dance pipe was passed around to all those who had been found worthy, a sign of their newfound redemption and new membership in the Sun Dance community.

The performance of a Sun Dance, which occurred almost annually, was prompted by the fulfillment of an individual vow, not by a fixed date on the ritual calandar. It was, as Leslie Spier notes, "not so much a thanks-offering as a new occasion for supplicating a supernatural power."[49] This power transformed the dancers as individuals as well as shaping them into a new community. It is because of this "transformation of the personality in the here and now" that Joseph Jorgensen believes that even the revival of the Sun Dance in this modern period is essentially a redemptive ritual.[50]

Transformative ritual poetry. Transformative rituals appeal to a vision of the end-time to bring about imminent, radical change in the social order, rather than in the individual. Because the imminence of the change is often announced by a prophet, such movements have often been called messianic. They have also been described as "revitalizing" movements because they attempt to "construct a more satisfying culture" than the present one, which is usually seen as laboring under poverty and oppression. Sometimes they have been called "nativistic" because the new world order they envision appears to be a call to return to the ancient, native ways that existed prior to subjugation. But according to David Aberle, all such transformative movements, however nuanced the distinctions, "view the process of change as cataclysmic, the time of change as imminent, the direction of change as teleologically guided, the appropriate supervision of the movement as charismatic, and at some point move to increase the separation of their members from the larger social sphere."[51] The Ghost Dance movement is the classic Native American example of such a transformative movement.

The Ghost Dance religion, which flourished during the 1880s, was killed by the Wounded Knee Massacre of 1890.[52] Its immediate motivation came from the totality of the Indian experience with whites, ranging from the initial acceptance to disillusionment and eventually defeat and exploitation. This experience precipitated a sense of despair during the reservation period, which in turn gave birth to a messianic vision, announced by the Paiute prophet Wovoka, which encompassed the destruction of the whites and the restoration of the Indians' natural exist-ence in all its fullness. At the time, the Ghost Dance was only the most recent and widespread example of a cultural pattern that responded to des-perate situations through a belief in a necessary apocalypse followed by a restoration of the world to its original, uncorrupted order.

Ghost Dance songs all had their origin in dreams, but they did not function as marks of individual identity. Rather they were shared, even exchanged, intertribally, thus becoming the property of the entire escha-tological community. Many Ghost Dance songs include statements from dead relatives about their imminent return to life, dance songs, and game songs, indicative of the nativistic temper of the movement. Some directly expressed the changed perspective on their relationship with whites, as these two Arapaho songs do:

I.

My children, when at first I liked the whites,
My children, when at first I liked the whites,
I gave them fruits,
I gave them fruits.

II.

Father, have pity on me,
Father, have pity on me;
I am crying for thirst,
I am crying for thirst;
All is gone—I have nothing to eat,
All is gone—I have nothing to eat.[53]

Others expressed the increasing urgency of the messianic apocalyptic vision that foretold a whirlwind and an upheaval of the earth that would bury the whites, return the land and the buffalo to the Indians, and restore their dead relatives. This is the theme of the following Sioux song:

I am coming in sight—Ehe 'ee 'ye!
I am coming in sight—Ehe 'ee 'ye!
I bring the whirlwind with me—E 'yahe 'eye!
I bring the whirlwind with me—E 'yahe 'eye!
That you may see each other—
That you may see each other.[54]

Set apart in their own ritual community, participating in the loosely framed, modular ritual of singing and the long, trance-like round dancing that gave the religion its name, the Indians believed they alone would be saved. The hoped-for apocalypse never came and white exploitation of Indian trust never ended.

In times of crises, when it looked as if the world as they knew it would end, Native Americans turned to ritual to reassert their faith in a transcendent power. "Ritual," Mircea Eliade observes, "is not only an optimistic vision of existence, but a total cleavage to being. By all his past behavior, religious man proclaims that he believes only in being, and that his participation in being is assured him by the primordial revelation of which he is a guardian."[55] Ritual enabled Native Americans, as it has other peoples, to externalize an inner vision of order and stability, and so to confront successfully the apparently arbitrary exercise of power manifested clearly in death, birth, epidemic illness, famine, and catastrophic change, in order to escape "the terror of history." And it is in ritual, where man exerts his greatest efforts to communicate with the sacred, that Native Americans exercise the major portion of their gift for oral poetry.

Although our attention must turn now to written literature, it is necessary to insist that oral tradition is today alive and well in Native American communities.[56] In some places, it is true, it has been altered greatly under the impact of acculturative forces; elsewhere, as in the pueblos, it is less altered. This is to be expected. Change is part of the dynamic of oral tradition. New genres have emerged, like Forty-Nine songs, which combine Indian and Anglo influences, and old ones, like the stories of the ever-relevant Trickster, remain popular. The advent of writing supplemented, but did not supplant, the oral culture.

Chapter Three

The Beginnings of a
Written Literature

From Invasion to Reservation

Painted in red on a peeled stick, the fortieth and final pictograph in the Lenni Lenape historical record known as the *Walam Olum* shows a curved shoreline and a sailing ship. The native language interpretation accompanying it translates: "Persons floating in from the East; the whites are coming." Tentative contacts between Native Americans and Europeans, principally for trade, had marked the century preceding the European invasion of America. But the invaders meant to transform this vast and alien land into a "new" England, "nieuw" Netherlands, or "nouveau" France, a vision they vigorously pursued with fateful consequences for the Lenni Lenape, whom they renamed the Delawares, and for other native peoples.[1]

With only a few notable exceptions like William Penn, English settlers were ambivalent toward Native Americans, whom they feared as military equals and yet demeaned as cultural inferiors. As a result, once the military effectiveness of Native peoples was considered to be neutralized, they became the object of intense acculturative efforts to transform them into the European's image of himself. Not long after the Puritans nearly annihilated the Pequots, for instance, they sent Eliot and Mayhew out to win souls for Christ and opened an Indian College at Harvard in 1656, but the project was doomed when "ungrateful" Indians rose up against them in King Philip's War (1675–76). This ambivalence was reflected in subsequent British and American Indian policy.

To replace the chaos of separate colonial initiatives, Britain adopted in 1755 a unified Indian policy, which regarded all Indian tribes as sovereign nations whose proper relationship to England and her subjects was to be set forth in treaties between representatives of the Crown and the tribes as heads of state. Following the American Revolution, and over the objections of the states, the federal government similarly assumed sole responsibility for treating with Indians. Specific authority in this regard was given to the Secretary of War, in whose department the Bureau of Indian Affairs was lodged from its creation in 1824 until its transfer to the new Department of the Interior in 1849.

Before the Revolution, Britain had created an Indian Territory from the Appalachian height of land to the Mississippi and closed it to colonial settlements. After the war, however, settlers entered the region and induced President Thomas Jefferson to adopt a gradualist policy in which agents and missionaries were charged with transforming Native Americans into citizen farmers in time to be assimilated into the advancing line of settlement. Following the War of 1812 the military superiority of the United States and the subsequent flood of immigration began to undermine this policy and encouraged the development in 1825 of a new Indian Territory farther west, beyond Missouri and Arkansas. When Andrew Jackson was inaugurated in 1829, he brought to Washington a view of Indians as mere "subjects of the United States" and despised treaty-making as "an absurdity." Under the weak pretense of saving the Indians from the onslaught of white settlers, he successfully muscled through Congress the Indian Removal Act of 1830, which provided for the removal to Indian Territory of whole Indian nations, many in devastating forced winter marches. He then attacked Indian sovereignty by refusing to enforce the Supreme Court's ruling in the Cherokee cases, which had reaffirmed that tribes were "domestic dependent nations" in a unique relationship to the federal government and not subject to state laws. By the time Jackson left office in 1837, most Native Americans between the Appalachians and the Mississippi had been removed to Indian Territory.

Frequently harried by unconfined tribes and subject to the continual traffic of westward emigrants whose routes transected their land, the tribes removed to Indian Territory were never really secure. Friction produced by such immigration, especially by the establishment of permanent mining communities, also brought a state of war to tribes surrounding Indian Territory. Although less well known than the post–Civil War conflicts, these military actions against tribes including the Cheyenne, Arapaho, and Utes established force as the prevalent method of dealing with Indian nations and compelled negotiations that expropriated more Indian land than in any other period. The Civil War also had two important consequences for Native American peoples. For the Cherokees and other tribes in the Indian Territory who had cast their lot with the Confederacy, the war's aftermath brought a series of punitive Reconstruction treaties. For the nonaligned tribes, the permanent militarization of the frontier by the incorporation of volunteer regiments into the regular army meant continued bitter fighting, especially after 1862, when the Confederate army no longer occupied the Union army in the west.

After the war, the federal government found itself in another internal debate over Indian policy. President Ulysses S. Grant adopted a "Peace Policy," assigning missionaries to replace spoils-system appointees as Indian agents, in hopes of pressing forward with acculturative efforts. But when divisions of authority, political favoritism, and religious discrimination vitiated the Peace Policy, the champions of force stepped in. Confident in the military might of the United States, Congress legislated the end of the treaty-making process in 1871, repudiating Indian sovereignty and subjecting tribes to congressional legislation and Executive Order. The army, meanwhile, following the pattern of Kit Carson's invasion of Navajoland, adopted a scorched-earth policy and executed a series of devastating winter campaigns. Many tribes, like the Kiowa and Comanche, witnessed their villages burned, their horse herds slaughtered, their guns taken away, their leaders sent off in chains to Florida without trial, and themselves removed to the Indian Territory. By 1880, such removals had forced sixty-seven tribes into an area only three-fourths the size of Oklahoma. Most of the rest had been confined to reservations elsewhere (see Figure 2).

Reservations appealed to almost everyone but Indians. Hardliners of the Jacksonian mold were found holding hands with Jeffersonian humanitarians. While the former wanted the Indians out of sight, if not out of mind, the latter fervently hoped the agent's staff of teacher, minister, doctor, and farmer would transform the Indians into literate and civil Christian agriculturalists. Formal education, modeled on the plan of Richard Pratt's Carlisle Indian School (1879), provided basic instruction and vocational training in a strict, pseudomilitary boarding school regimen (removal from the "bad influence" of resistive parents was thought desirable). As acculturative mechanisms, however, reservations failed for many reasons: the obvious corruption of agents who profited from mishandling annuity monies; the physical and cultural impediments to establishing an agricultural economy; the intrusion of outsiders who came to compete for Indian land, resources, and treaty benefits; and general repudiation of federal management in Indian affairs. Another reason, Arrell Gibbson argues, is that Indians critically judged "the relative merits of the Anglo-American culture they were expected, even required to accept. Most adult Indians found it pietistic, legalistic, obsessively materialistic, and downright unattractive."[2]

The disastrous consequences of humanitarianism were played out a second time in the 1880s, when "Friends of the Indian" began calling atten-

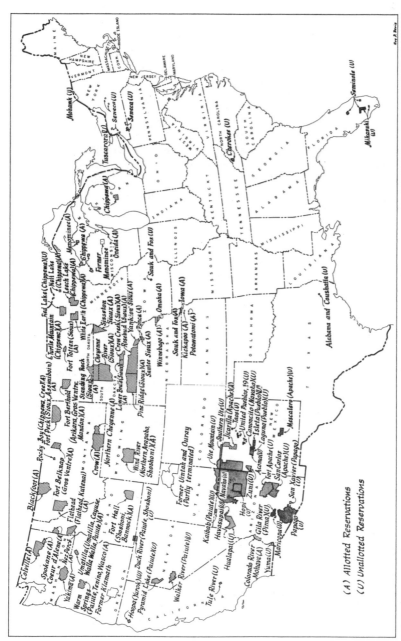

Figure 2. Indian Reservations in the "Lower 48," 1969

tion to the failure of reservations and demanded reform. The popular outcry was raised most loudly by Helen Hunt Jackson, whose *Century of Dishonor* (1881) and *Ramona* (1884) raged against the dehumanization of the reservation system. The solution of the reformers was a radical yoking of the current environmental determinism with traditional Jeffersonianism. One could undermine the Indians' communal base of tribal culture and economy, the argument went, by forcibly imposing private property through partitioning the reservation into family and individual allotments; then the transformation into individualized Christian agriculturalists must surely follow. In 1887 Congress passed the General Allotment or Dawes Act, which ordered that every reservation be surveyed into 160-acre parcels and the name of every tribal member recorded on a tribal roll. Reservation land was then allotted a parcel to a family, a half-parcel to an individual (no land was set aside for unborn children), and the remaining land put up for sale. Allotted Indians became citizens of the United States and subject to state or territorial laws. The Burke Act (1906) ended this automatic conferral of citizenship, however. It also removed the few safeguards restricting the sale of allotted land and transferred responsibility for probating estates of the Five Civilized Tribes from the federal to the county courts. In the widespread corruption that followed, Indians were pauperized. When the first European set foot in the Western Hemisphere, Native Americans held almost 3 billion acres of land. When the Dawes Act was passed in 1887, treaties and usurpations had reduced that holding to only 150 million acres. And when it was finally repealed in 1934, Indians were left with only 48 million acres, or 1.5 percent of their original land. Despite this steady loss of rights, land, and cultural autonomy, the Indians slowly developed some effective literary spokesmen.

Nonfiction

Religious and political writing.   Many of the Native Americans educated in the seventeenth century at Harvard Indian College have left their mark on history in other than literary ways. James Printer, for instance, at one time John Eliot's principal interpreter, stood at King Philip's side during the latter's struggle and translated native demands into English, even having a part in the famed captivity of Mary Rowlandson. But except for a few letters, signatures on correspondence, and occasional mention in historical documents, they left no written record. It was not for lack of education. Caleb Chaesahteamuk, a Natick and the first Native American college graduate, was fluent in English, Hebrew, Greek, and

Latin when he gave his 1665 Harvard commencement address in the latter tongue. In the backlash of King Philip's War, however, Harvard closed its Indian College in 1693, and those who had spent some time there found more practical employment as schoolteachers, interpreters, and even as mariners and carpenters.[3]

In 1754, Eleazar Wheelock opened Moor's Charity School in Lebanon, Connecticut. One of his students was Samson Occum (1723–92), a young, semiliterate Christian Mohegan. In four years Occum completed the customary classical education with training in English and the scriptural languages, but, as one observer noted, his talent lay in his oratory, which, especially before Indians, was "natural and free and eloquent, quick and powerful."[4] In 1766 Wheelock engaged Occum to preach in England, knowing his sermons would draw attention to the school's accomplishments and raise funds. Largely on the basis of funds raised on Occum's tour, Wheelock removed to New Hampshire, where he founded Dartmouth College. Occum himself was soon impoverished, angered by being refused a license to preach (a common complaint of Indian preachers), and embittered with what he felt was Wheelock's betrayal of the Indians' cause.

In 1771, Occum was called to preach a sermon on the execution of Moses Paul, an Indian who while intoxicated had bludgeoned to death a leading citizen of Waterbury. Occum's sermon not only painted for Moses Paul the fires of hell that awaited him if he did not repent; it also affirmed, for the many Indians in the congregation who had come to hear him speak, the evils of drunkenness and the extent to which their lives and their communities had been disrupted by rum. Occum published his address, which went through at least nineteen editions, becoming something of a bestseller. He followed this with a collection of hymns. Many of them are clearly garnered from elsewhere, but a few for which no source has been found may be attributable to him. These march along in the steady doggerel meters of the Michael Wigglesworth tradition:

> Come all my young Companions Come,
> To hear me boldly tell,
> The Wonders of Redeeming Love,
> That Save's my Soul from Hell.[5]

Samson Occum spent the rest of his life in service to the Brotherton Indians, a remnant community of New England Indians, including his own Mohegan kinsmen, which had removed to Oneida country in New York State.

A native writer who had much more impact than Samson Occum, and the first really to explore the medium of written English, was William Apes, a Pequot (b. 1798). During the 1830s, when Andrew Jackson was enforcing a policy of Indian Removal and public consideration of Indian rights ebbed to a low-water mark, Apes became the most vocal Native American advocate of his people's rights in the North. An itinerant Methodist preacher who had made several circuits of New England, Apes visited the Wampanoags at Mashpee on Cape Cod in 1833 and became involved in their efforts to regain control over their own affairs, which had been placed in the hands of a Board of Overseers who were clearly abusing their trust. With the support of reform-minded Boston newspaper editor Benjamin Hallett, Apes became the voice of the Indian rights advocates in the Mashpee community who sought, and in 1834 won, the right to incorporate themselves into a township, to elect their own selectmen, and otherwise carry on the business of self-government. In a pamphlet entitled "Indian Nullification of the Unconstitutional Laws of Massachusetts Relative to the Marshpee Tribe" (1835), Apes carefully outlined the history of the conflict. In the face of Jackson's removal of the southern tribes, Apes published in 1836 his boldly titled *Eulogy on King Philip,* in which he asserted that the "national rights of all Indian tribes should be respected within a White society, thus obviating the necessity of removing Indians beyond the pale of civilization and settlement."[6] After 1836 Apes faded from public view, and the circumstances of his death are not known. The same cannot be said for his youth, however, for he authored the first Native American autobiography.

The autobiographical tradition.   Indian autobiographies can be usefully divided into two categories: those written by the hand of a literate Native American and those others, customarily called "as-told-to" autobiographies, dictated by an unschooled Native American to a literate person who did the actual writing. Both types occur at the very beginnings of a written Native American literature in English. Contrary to expectations, the written autobiography of William Apes preceded into print by four years the earliest "as-told-to" autobiography, that of Black Hawk.

The first part of William Apes's *A Son of the Forest* (1829)[7] is an incredible story of brutality and hardship. After claiming descent from King Philip, "though not with a view of appearing great in the eyes of others" (7), he describes being so badly beaten at four by his drunken grandparents, with whom he was staying following his parents' separation, that he had to be supported at public expense by the town of Colchester, Connecticut, for the full year his wounds required to heal. As an abandoned child he was then formally bound over by the town to the staunch Baptist family that had first taken him in after his beating. There he learned to read and write, having six years of formal schooling; to love church, which he attended devotedly; and to fear his fellow Native Americans—a term he insisted upon instead of "Indians"—because of the frontier horror stories he had been told. After a childhood of being alternately beaten and cajoled, he ran away at age eleven, and his indenture was sold for the first time. He ran away from his third and last bondholder to join the army and fight in the War of 1812 in defense of Plattsburg.

His experience of personal prejudice was compounded by the army's institutional prejudice. Not only did the army violate the terms of his enlistment, but when his service ended he was not given the bonus pay or section of land awarded to the Anglo-American soldiers at whose side he had fought. As a native he was further distressed that the government "would claim our services in cases of perilous national emergency, and still deny us the right of citizenship" (66). After the war he held a series of odd jobs, during one of which he confronted an employer who wanted to deprive him of his pay: "I had been cheated so often that I determined to have my right this time, and ever after" (79). Still feeling at age twenty a call to deeper Christianity, he was baptized a Methodist in December 1818 and found new purpose in his emerging power as a preacher. Although originally opposed for preaching without a license, he began to preach in the Providence area, where he was eventually licensed and developed a good reputation, and then made several circuits of New England. With this apparent vindication of his calling, his story concludes.

The appearance of Apes's autobiography and of Indian autobiographies as a genre coincided with the emergence of American autobiography. The two traditions differed significantly, however, as Arnold Krupat has observed. In contrast to American autobiographies, which were "old-world oriented and self-consciously literary . . . includ[ing] scenes of writing (and reading) important to self-definition," Native American autobiographies derived from oral tradition, however spoiled by a "fall into writing."[8] But even within the Native American autobiographical tradition there are important consequences related to the nature of this "fall." As far as one can tell, for instance, Apes's autobiography is entirely the product of his own mind and hand, in contrast to the collaboration that produced, and in the production altered, Black Hawk's narrative. Apes's autobiography established a pattern of personal history in which Christianity and education cooperated to free the Indian from his tribal past, which was viewed in the light of prevailing cultural determinism as an impediment to "civilization" and the locus of intercultural and interracial antagonism. Thus, the very education that enables Apes to write his own story also displaces him from that culture of his parents and grandparents to which he seeks to testify. This problem of point of view is even more acute for Black Hawk and other non-literate Indians, for whom the production of their narrative required the surrender of one's testimony into the hands of a writer, and perhaps also a translator, who gave not only texture but form to a story they pretended was not theirs.

In 1832 Black Hawk, the Sauk leader who had refused to submit to the removal of his people across the Mississippi, was the object of a fifteen-week campaign of confusion, catastrophe, and bitterness known as the Black Hawk War. The next year he wanted the opportunity to tell his story. John Patterson, a local newspaper editor, testified that he had "written this work according to the dictation of Black Hawk, through the United States' Interpreter Antoine LeClair," and consequently could not consider himself "responsible for any of the facts, or views contained in it."[9] The facts are, despite Patterson's disclaimer, for the most part accurate, but the language in which they are expressed is often suspiciously latinate.

Raised to prominence at the beginning of the nineteenth century through a success in war, Black Hawk inherited his people's medicine bundle when his father was killed in a fight against Cherokees. In 1804 a party of four Sauks, visiting St. Louis in the hope of securing the release of one of their people arrested for killing an American, signed away all Sauk land east of the Mississippi. They returned home with little memory of the event, having been intoxicated most of the time. Then in 1812 doubtful American trade policies succeeded, where the Shawnee prophet had failed, in bringing the impoverished Sauk into the war on the side of the British. While leading a party of warriors against Detroit, Black Hawk was replaced at home as war chief by Keokuk, who had never killed a man. After the war, when the invasion of settlers and predations of alcohol had precipitated a crisis, Black Hawk successfully resisted the removal of his band to Iowa, despite the dissension caused by Keokuk, who divided the people against him with his "smooth tongue" (121). Black Hawk then expressed a willingness to make a fair financial settlement for the land, but the authorities responded with force. Turned off the land and disappointed in the British refusal to come to his aid, he prepared to surrender, but his negotiating party was attacked. After a series of evasions and skirmishes, the Black Hawk "War" concluded when he was forced to surrender following the Battle of the Bad Axe, where not only his warriors but women and

children were killed trying to cross the Mississippi. Put in chains and tak-
en east to meet President Jackson, he toured several major cities before
being set free and returned, humiliatingly, into the custody of Keokuk. As
Black Hawk tells his story, his life is one continuous struggle against pred-
atory Americans and his nemesis Keokuk, who was "willing to barter our
rights merely for the good opinion of the whites; and cowardly enough to
desert our village to them" (121). Throughout, his own perspective is that
the lies, threats, and actions of others compelled him to use force rather
than follow his own reasonable inclination to negotiate.

Both strands of the autobiographical tradition were sustained through
the remainder of the nineteenth century. In 1847, George Copway (Ojibwa) published the autobiography he wrote, *The Life History and Travels of
Kah-Ge-Ga-Bowh,* which went through several printings. An otherwise
conventional story of a "redeemed Indian" it differs from Apes's earlier
work and later nineteenth-century written autobiographies such as Andrew Blackbird's *History of Ottawa and Chippewa Indians . . . And a Personal
Family History of the Author* (1887) by having immersed the life history in
the context of tribal history. In the early reservation period, George Bird
Grinnell recorded "as-told-to" autobiographies among the Cheyennes. But
two unrelated events at the beginning of this century focused new attention on both of these forms; one was the general popularity of Charles Eastman's autobiographical works and the other, a new emphasis in modern
anthropology.

Autobiographies written by Native Americans became enormously popular as a result of three volumes published by Charles Eastman (Santee
Sioux). The most conventionally autobiographical of these, *From the Deep
Woods to Civilization* (1916), describes the years of his formal education to
and professional participation in Anglo-American culture. Written fifteen
to twenty years after he graduated from college, these books reflect Eastman's ambivalence toward both cultures of which he was a part. He was
set on the white man's road by his father, who returned from Canada, having been thought long dead, to tell his son of the wonders of civilization.
To become citizen Indians, the Eastmans were required to renounce their
tribal ties in order to homestead near Flandreau, South Dakota. From mission school there, Charles was sent to Albert Riggs's Santee Normal School
in Nebraska. Later, as he was about to depart Santee for Beloit College,
Eastman received news of his father's death, "less than three months after
Custer's gallant command was annihilated by hostile Sioux."[10] Already he
had developed the idealized view of "Christian civilization" that was later
to disappoint him bitterly: "I saw it as the development of every natural

resource; the broad brotherhood of mankind; the blending of all languages and gathering of all races under one religious faith . . . we must quit the forest trail for the breaking plow. . . ."[11] In the fall of 1883, he entered Dartmouth College, and four years later, Boston Medical School.

At graduation in 1890, he took a commission in the Indian Service, which posted him to Pine Ridge in time to bury the dead and tend the injured on both sides following the Wounded Knee massacre. When agents defrauded the Sioux of their compensation, Eastman objected loudly, but his protests could not alter the whitewash, and he resigned. Having recently married Elaine Goodale, he tried to set up private practice in St. Paul, but shortly was induced to begin a life of service to the national Indian community, first by establishing YMCA associations in Indian communities and then as a lobbyist in Washington, where his visits to the slums of eastern cities confirmed his repugnance for American materialism. His support of the Boy Scout Indian programs and his public appearance in tribal dress, though they did reinforce the "noble savage" stereotype, were Eastman's attempts to assert the dignity of native culture in terms compatible with the best elements of Christianity in his emerging universalist perspective.

Though Eastman himself referred to *Indian Boyhood* (1902) as the preliminary volume of his autobiography, from another perspective, *The Soul of the Indian* (1911) also served that purpose. The first is a nonchronological and often generalized collection of observations about hunting customs, games, storytelling, and so on, which he combined with anecdotal reminiscences of his childhood. Very popular among citybound Anglo youth in the first decades of this century, *Indian Boyhood* had an enormous impact on Boy Scouting and the "Indian hobbyist" movement, and is still in print today. In *The Soul of the Indian* Eastman addressed the parents of those children reading *Indian Boyhood*. Disgruntled by the materialistic Babbitts around them, they lionized Eastman for his universalist, romanticized outlook. Deeply convinced himself of the value of tribal religion as he knew it, Eastman nevertheless did not distinguish among different tribal cultures. This led many of his readers to assume wrongly that vision quests, individualistic religious experiences, solitude, and "spiritual communion with his brothers in the animal kingdom"[12] were the common denominators of a universal Indian spirituality. He strengthened his appeal by contrasting Indian religion, which he implicitly identified with "real Christianity," with the "professionalism of the pulpit." Indian religion was more natural because it was universal, nonsectarian, and had a prior existence in time; it was also superior, because it was not compromised, being neither derived from something earlier nor encumbered by ulterior motivations. The popularity of the Eastman format, which combined both autobiography and commentary, spurred similar works, notably those by Luther Standing Bear (Sioux) and James Paytiamo (Acoma). Prompted by an anthropologist, Don Talayesva (Hopi) produced an autobiography that was later edited and published. John Joseph Mathews's *Talking to the Moon* is a lyrical account of his life in the Osage country of Oklahoma. Recent authors of written autobiographies include Kay Bennett (Navajo), Anna Moore Shaw (Pima), and Refugio Savala (Yaqui). The unique contribution of N. Scott Momaday (Kiowa) to this tradition will be treated in chapter 6.

Just as Eastman's works generated a popular audience for written autobiographies, the activity of anthropologists in collecting "life histories" renewed interest in "as-told-to" autobiographies in the first decades of this century. In this first group Paul Radin's *Autobiography of a Winnebago Indian* (1920) is something of a classic. But it was in the 1930s that anthropologists recorded the largest number of "as-told-to" autobiographies, some of which have become well known not only as social documents and successful collaborations but as remarkable literary works, especially the autobiographies of Maria Chona (Papago) and Left-Handed (Navajo). More recent "as-told-to" autobiographies have been dictated by Mountain Wolf Woman (Winnebago), Helen Sekaquaptewa (Hopi), James Sewid (Kwakiutl), Rosalio Moises (Yaqui), and Frank Mitchell (Navajo). The single most influential "as-told-to" autobiography languished for thirty years, however, until it was resurrected in the more receptive climate of the 1960s.

This was *Black Elk Speaks, Being the Life Story of a Holy Man of the Oglala Sioux, as told through John G. Neihardt* (1932; rpt. 1961). Neihardt, a poet with an epic vision of the passing of the West, shaped the narrative around the issue that Black Elk himself emphasized: his failure to live up to the vision that had been entrusted to him. The first, and most carefully told, part of the story begins when at age nine Black Elk received an extraordinarily complex and beautiful vision that showed how he would lead his nation through four difficult periods until, in the face of starvation and cultural disintegration, he found the four-colored herb that would revitalize his people. Although his people were even then fighting the great battles of the 1870s with the Americans, he suppressed his vision for fear of being ridiculed, and to this he attributed the cause of his and his people's subsequent tragedies. A turning point occurred at age seventeen, when, after the confinement of the Oglalas to the reservation and Crazy Horse's surrender, he felt compelled to tell his father his vision. After it was acted out for him, his healing power became manifest and he assumed the role of a medicine man. Despite the good he was accomplishing with individuals, Black Elk realized that his vision medicine was for the nation as a whole. The last act of the story commences when he joins Buffalo Bill's Wild West Show, hoping to find in his travels some key to unlock the mystery of the white man's power and so rescue his people, but he is disappointed. His ultimate despair is assured when he aligns himself with the Ghost Dancers, witnesses the massacre at Wounded Knee and the starvation of the refugees, and is himself wounded in the aftermath.

Although it is well known that the language of the text is Neihardt's, it is also true that Neihardt added some material to the narrative, including the final two paragraphs ("A people's dream died there. It was a beautiful dream").[13] Neihardt argued that these words represented only what Black Elk "would have said if he had been able," and that he had been faithful to Black Elk's tone throughout. In the collaborative effort that is Black Elk's autobiography, the powerful appeals that Arnold Krupat identified as the energies at work in "bicultural composite authorship" achieved their greatest effect.

The historical and ethnographic traditions.   In the elaborate corpus of oral tradition, Native American peoples did not distinguish among political, religious, military, or other kinds of history. Similarly, the first histories written by Native Americans tell their stories in a holistic manner. The first such history, *Sketches of Ancient History of the Six Nations* (1827), was written by David Cusick (Tuscarora).[14] Following a pattern to which many subsequent native-authored histories would conform, Cusick opened his narrative with a traditional creation story, in this case, the Woman Who Fell from the Sky (see chapter 1). This he followed with monster-slaying episodes from the heroic past; the dispersion and linguistic differentiation of the Iroquois; their rivalries and warfare; and finally the planting of the Great Tree of Peace and founding of the League of the Iroquois. Although neither skillfully written nor historically accurate by Western standards, Cusick's narrative is nonetheless a remarkably sustained first effort. Recent scholarship has made important claims for the accuracy of Ojibwa histories written later in the century by George Copway (1850), Peter Jones (1861), William Whipple Warren (1885), and Andrew Blackbird (1887).[15] A modern work remarkable for its oral character and historical interest is *Cheyenne Memories* (1967), dictated to Margot Liberty by John Stands-in-Timber, an acknowledged tribal historian over eighty years old, who prodded his memory with a cache of documents, newspaper clippings, and other memorabilia.

Although the American reading public may have been attracted to the study of native cultures by Schoolcraft's *Algic Researches* (1839), which Longfellow pillaged for his *Song of Hiawatha* (1855), Native people focused their energies on ethnography as a result of experiencing enormous changes in their own cultures. In this regard Peter Jones's Ojibwa history is significant for also being the first Native-authored ethnography. In place of an explicit chronological framework for his history, Jones offered topical chapters such as "Courtship and Marriage," "War," and "Their Religion." Yet he felt justified in calling his pioneering work "history" because he could demonstrate in each of these areas the changes resulting from white influence. Later, in 1881, Elias Johnson (Tuscarora) published his *Legends, Traditions and Laws of the Iroquois.* Soon other Native Americans were working closely with anthropologists. George Hunt (Kwakiutl) contributed more than 6,000 manuscript pages to Franz Boas's work with that people. Francis LaFlesche was adopted by Alice Fletcher, who encouraged his interest, directed his education, and collaborated with him in describing his Osage culture. While he was a streetcar conductor in New Jersey, J. N. B. Hewitt (Tuscarora) was enlisted by Erminie Smith to assist her in her work and became a premier Iroquoianist in his own right. Others in the first class of native anthropologists included Arthur C. Parker (Seneca) and William Jones (Fox). Heading a later generation were Ella Deloria (Dakota) and Edward P. Dozier (Santa Clara Pueblo).[16]

Early Native American Poetry

In the nineteenth century Native Americans began to write poetry in English for publication, most of which was based on the models to which they had been exposed in their formal education. Some, like the Creek poet Alex Posey, must certainly have experienced a tension deriving from the attempt to accommodate native conceptions to an alien language and verse forms. Struggling to retain—or perhaps in the case of John Rollin Ridge, striving to reject—those distinctive nuances of aesthetic value they believed to be peculiarly tribal, all felt an awkward disjuncture between their poetic and cultural identities.

The first Native American to publish a volume of poetry was John Rollin Ridge (Cherokee). As a child he had witnessed the assassination of his father, John Ridge, by members of the Ross party, and his mother, fearing for their lives, removed the family to Arkansas. After attending Great Barrington (Massachusetts) School, he returned to the Cherokee Nation but moved to Missouri shortly after his marriage because the political situation

again threatened his life. From Missouri he left with the goldseekers heading for California. He arrived there in 1850, and after a series of odd jobs
took up newspaper editing and writing. In a letter to Stand Watie, he
wrote that he wanted to "establish a newspaper devoted to advancing Indian rights and interests" that would "bring into its columns not only the
fire of my own pen, such as it may be, but the contributions of the leading
minds of different Indian nations."[17] Such a paper would certainly have had
a tremendous impact, equal to or greater than that of the Cherokee *Phoenix,* which had been edited by Watie's brother, Elias Boudinot, but it never materialized. And such an interest in Indian issues is not reflected in
Ridge's *Poems,* published in 1868, two years after his death.[18]

The bulk of Ridge's verse concerns his romantic relations with various
women whom he idealized. There is such a quantity of this unembarrassed
fantasizing throughout the volume as to make it very sappy wood indeed.
Though some of it certainly has an autobiographical basis and is probably
the more fawning in just that proportion, part of it seems to be a generalized expression of the Muse theme imbued with Romantic lights. "Erin-
na," for instance, is addressed to a supposedly historical incarnation of this
almost Poe-like vision of supernal beauty. Even when he tries to inject
racial and historical tensions into a situation, as in "The Stolen White
Girl," he founders on breakers of anapestic sentiment: "Though he stole
her away from the land of the whites, / Pursuit is in vain, for her bosom
delights / In the love she bears the dark-eyed, the proud" (72–73). Occasionally his imagination bestirs itself to more exotic environs, as in "A
Scene along the Rio de Las Plumas," where he concocts a poetic stew of
languorous lilies, slinking serpents, and other jungle phantasmagoria.
However conventional, these are some of his more interesting poems, if
only because the picturesque has the virtue of novelty that sentiment lacks.

Ridge also attempted to write in an epic vein, which he mined in two
directions. He was impressed by the West's many natural wonders and
wrote poems cataloging the marvels of his adopted state. Most of these,
like "Mt. Shasta," are marked by the rapturous tones one expects from a
romantic sensibility for the sublime: "golden-sanded streams" wend their
way amid "the yellow largesse of the waving field," while that "tower of
pride," Mt. Shasta, "stands / Imperial amid the lesser heights" (13–16).
But in each of these poems, and others written for public readings on special occasions such as Independence Day, he thematically linked the settlement of the West with the progress of civilization. Although he was a
Native American, in this he could not be distinguished from his Anglo-
American contemporaries, most of whom subscribed to the belief that his-

tory everywhere followed a universal process: hunting and gathering societies were succeeded by pastoral ones, which eventually gave way to the agricultural societies, from which art, science, and civilization had sprung. In a paean to the march of technological civilization, "The Atlantic Cable," Indians and other "skin-clad" multitudes wait in the dark world for the "dawn of letters" and the "light of science." Elsewhere, in a poem written for public declamation on July 4, 1861, he praised Andrew Jackson and "victory-blest" Cortez as heroes of civilization, although only one year earlier he had compared Aztec Mexico to England in the time of Alfred the Great, and pressed his readers: "Were peace and plenty but the Spaniard's right? / The Aztec *barbarous* because not *white?*" (119, emphasis original). And although he also praised Incan social order as the epitome of equitable communal living, this idealization, carrying all the connotations of its strong agrarian message, does not temper the force of his condemnation of "skin-clad" natives.

Ridge was a competent versifier in the popular romantic mold, but he was hardly original and seldom matched the achievements of those whose work he imitated. Alternating in tone between strident bombast and debilitating pathos, he bewailed his aspiration toward and failure to achieve a vision of ideal beauty, and harped on the march of progress across a continent of unmatched sublimity. These themes, already clichés in his time, he further burdened with stock metrical schemes. Yet despite this mediocrity, Ridge was able to establish himself as a literary figure in San Francisco alongside the likes of Bret Harte, Mark Twain, and Joaquin Miller.

Alexander Posey was born in Indian Territory in 1873 the son of Lewis Posey, a Scots-Irish former United States marshal, and Pohas Harjo (Nancy Phillips), a member of the oldest Creek family. Until he was twelve Posey spoke only Creek, but his father insisted on education and English, so the boy received private tutoring before entering the grade school in Eufala. He went on to Bacone Indian University, where he set type for the faculty newspaper, in which he published his first poems. In 1895, the year of his graduation, he was elected to the Creek legislature and in the following year was appointed superintendent of the Creek Orphanage. This was only the first in a series of appointments in education for the most learned man among the Creeks, but he left that field for his first love, writing. Although as editor of the *Indian Journal* and *Muskogee Times* he satirized both sides of the allotment issue in his Fus Fixico letters (see below), he was convinced that enrolling every last eligible person was the only way for the Creeks to retain their land, and in 1905 he joined the Creek Enrollment party. That same year he served as secretary of the convention to draw up a constitution for the proposed state of Sequoyah and was the document's principal author. He drowned on May 23, 1908, while trying to cross a rain-swollen river. Two years later his wife brought out his *Collected Poems*.[19]

Alex Posey believed that "the Indian talks in poetry, . . . but in attempting to write in English he is handicapped," and sought for himself his tribal poetry's "power and ability to express in sonorous musical phrases . . . gorgeous word-pictures" (62). At a very early stage in his career, he valued the imagery and music that seemed to give poetry its magic. Although he shared with Ridge and E. Pauline Johnson the burden of the vocabulary of sentiment he inherited from his models, he differed from them in being a consummate musician who successfully avoided the galloping jangle of most Poe-imitators. Instead he shifted among slant and eye rhymes and experimented with a range of metrical schemes, seeking some way to lean lightly on the wind and fit his voice to a melody:

> O Twilight, fold me, let me rest within
> Thy dusky wings;
> For I am weary, weary. Lull me with
> Thy whisperings,
> So tender; let my sleep be fraught with dreams
> of beauteous things.
>
> (115)

When through some good fortune he found a rougher language than the satin speech to which he was accustomed, it merged with this subtle, searching music to create vital poetry, as in this image of "July":

> The air without has taken fever;
> Fast I feel the beating of its pulse.
> The leaves are twisted on the maple,
> In the corn the autumn's premature.
>
> (106)

However colored by his education, Posey's Indianness, unlike that of Ridge, was central to his conception of himself and of his poetry. Although most of his subjects were stock elements in popular romanticism, Posey differed from his contemporaries in attempting to endow the landscape with some sense of its Indian history. In titles he addressed the winds, mountains, rivers, and settlements by their Creek names. He took pride in his people and celebrated illustrious figures in verse. His lyrical elegy of Col. D. N. McIntosh sings with resonances of Whitman: "Oh, carol, carol early thrush. . ." (127). His "Ode to Sequoyah" marches in stately, modulated iambics:

> The names of Watie and Boudinot—
> The valiant warrior and gifted sage—
> And other Cherokees, may be forgot,
> But thy name shall descend to every age.
>
> (184)

Yet reality seems to have been busy forever confounding Posey's ideals. Swelled with a sense of pride in the international position of the United States and captivated by its Big Brother foreign policy, he wrote unashamedly that America's "dawn lights up the armored front / In Cuba and the Phillipines" (105). But he was not so easily deceived at home. A few years later, when the army had captured and imprisoned Chitto Harjo for opposing the allotment process and Posey's enrollment commission as the final despoliation of the Creek nation, Posey boldly published his respect: "He is the noble red man still. / Condemn him and his kind to shame / I bow to him, exalt his name!" (88). Of the three nineteenth-century native poets, Posey distinguished himself not only for the varied music of his verse but for the clarity of vision and deep personal engagement he brought to the act of writing.

Less gifted and less political than Posey, E. Pauline Johnson (Tekahionwake) was born in Brantsford, Ontario, in 1862, the daughter of the chief of the Mohawk nation, which had removed to Canada after the Revolutionary War, in which their famed leader, Joseph Brant, had allied his people with the British. As a child she met Edward, Prince of Wales, the Duke of Connaught, and other dignitaries who visited her father's estate, which was elegantly furnished with a piano, silver and china, and a fine library. Although Johnson had only some home tutoring and a few years of elementary school, she read widely, including all of Scott and Longfellow and most of Byron and Shakespeare, by the time she was twelve. The stunning success of her first platform reading at age thirty set her on a career of public performances that took her to England and the United States and all over Canada, crossing the Rockies nineteen times. When she died in 1913, her health broken by incessant touring, she was a national literary figure in Canada and the most widely celebrated Native American poet.[20] Her three books of poetry were collected in a volume she had titled *Flint and Feather* but which was published posthumously in 1917.[21] Much of her poetry has a rhetorical flourish that must surely have been heightened with each public reading. She wrote comfortably in a variety of conventional metrical schemes and did not restrict herself to a particular theme, writing even religious verse. Most of her poetry, however, is concerned with natural or historical subjects.

Despite lapses into pathetic fallacy, her poems on natural subjects, such as "Marshlands," are often attractive for their painterly effect:

> A thin wet sky that yellows at the rim,
> And meets with sun-lost lip the marsh's brim
> . . . . :. . . .
>
> Late cranes with heavy wing, and lazy flight
> Sail up the silence with the nearing night.
>   (42)

Moved by the playing of a European violinist who had visited Canada, she tried her hand in "Autumn Orchestra" at using sound rather than color to paint a scene, so that oaks march through their stanza sonorously, aspens sing at "sweet high treble," and the hare-bell "chimes all day long." In pieces like this, and the acrostic "Brandon," one of several poems she wrote as tributes to different cities in which she had read, she proved herself an able versifier.

Her poems about Indians, however, were highly romanticized. She exceeded Posey and even Ridge as a master of narrative poetry, writing melodramatic verses, some with dialogue, of chases and captures that must have thrilled her audiences. She frequently wrote about intertribal conflicts, especially those between the Huron and her own people, but these and other topics were part of a glorious past that featured "braves" with "haughty and defiant eye" who "bend to death—but never to disgrace" (4). One of her most famous poems, and her first publicly recited work, "A Cry From an Indian Wife," suggested that in the armed struggle for the land that would become Canada, mothers on both sides grieved not only for the loss of their own sons but for those of the other side as well. In this poem, and in others like "The Cattle Thief," in which an Indian is caught killing cattle to support his starving family, she strove to make a point about the injustices done to Indians. Her final attitude, however, is ambiguous, her sadness neutralized by resignation, and her anger's edge dulled by divided loyalties. Of the British, to whom her people had been loyal for nearly two hundred years, she writes as if only a reminder were needed to restore justice:

> . . . their new rule and council is well meant.
> They but forget we Indians owned the land . . .

She concludes fatalistically:

> Though starved, crushed, plundered, lies our nation low . . .
> Perhaps the white man's God has willed it so.
>
> (14, 17)

In the end, E. Pauline Johnson became most famous not for speaking of Indian rights but for romanticizing the woodland Indian, especially in her "canoe songs," idylls of a dream.

Toward a Native American Fiction

Possibly the first piece of native-authored fiction was *Poor Sarah, or Religion Exemplified in the Life and Death of an Indian Woman*, a sketch published in pamphlet form in 1823 and attributed to Elias Boudinot, a Cherokee.[22] A staunch Presbyterian and one of the first Cherokees to have a thorough formal education, Boudinot would become more famous at a later date for being the founding editor of the Cherokee *Phoenix*, the first native newspaper and a bilingual one at that. The sketch consists of several scenes, narrated by an educated white woman, that tell of her relationship to Sarah, an impoverished Indian, whose simple faith, spoken in a very credible broken English, interiorly convicts the sophisticated narrator of hypocrisy. Because at the time of the pamphlet's publication Boudinot was teaching at a Cherokee mission school, he may have written the sketch for the double purpose of demonstrating that Indians were amenable to proselytizing and to education, and at the same time to prick the consciences of easterners, such as the New Englanders he knew from his Connecticut school days, who thought themselves inherently superior to Indians. Because he had signed the treaty supporting removal to Indian Territory, Boudinot was assassinated in 1839 by followers of the Principal Cherokee Chief, John Ross.

Unlike Boudinot's thinly disguised religious tract, John Rollin Ridge's *Life and Adventures of Joaquin Murieta* (1854) was the first piece of fiction authored by a Native American for the purposes of entertainment.[23] One might speculate upon vicarious revenge as a deeper motivation, since Ridge's father was killed in the same spate of assassinations that took Boudinot's life. Murieta, his folk hero, is motivated by his experience of prejudice, Mexicans being "looked upon as no better than conquered subjects of the United States, having no rights which could stand before a haughtier and superior race" (9). Forced from his mining claims and his farm by abusive Anglos, even compelled to witness the rape of his beloved, he nevertheless resists outlawry until his half-brother is killed without a trial by a mob accusing him of stealing horses. Only then, when "wanton cruelty and the tyranny of prejudice had reached their climax" (12), did he "declare to a friend that he would live henceforth for revenge and that his path would be marked with blood" (12–13). True to his word, the remainder of the tale is a breathless succession of robberies, murders, mutilations, and shootouts, until fate delivers Joaquin into the hands of Capt. Harry Love, an equal "whose brain was as strong and clear in the midst of dangers as that of the daring robber among whom he was sent" (146). Although Ridge's fictionalization of the bandit's life is practically without form, the simplicity of the characterization and its relentless energy made it enormously popular, giving California its first folk-hero and adding a new face to the ranks of dime-novel desperadoes.

After Ridge's novelization of Murieta's life, several decades passed before the publication of fiction in English by Native Americans resumed in earnest. One possible explanation for this hiatus is that the readers of popular magazines, accustomed to a steady diet of stories of Indian depravity associated with the wars of the 1870s, were not prepared emotionally or ideologically to accept literature that treated Indian themes positively. This attitude did not begin to change until the late 1880s and early 1890s with the publication of Helen Hunt Jackson's work and the disclosures about the Wounded Knee tragedy. Then Indian authors like Eastman began to publish autobiographical works that presented native cultures and values in a positive light. A more tangible reason is that few Indians had sufficient English language instruction to make an attempt at, to say nothing of careers in, writing and publishing. By the turn of the century that, too, was beginning to change, as a few of the Indian students who completed elementary schooling went on to higher education. With a degree from Dartmouth (Eastman), Stanford (Oskison), Earlham College (Zitkala-Sa), or Bacone (Posey), they often found themselves, whether by inclination or community pressures, in positions of leadership in Indian affairs where not a few saw the advantage of dramatizing Indian issues through fiction.

Alex Posey, the Creek poet, knew what was percolating in the heart of his own Creek Nation, which just a few years past the turn of the century was anticipating statehood for Indian Territory and coping with allotment. Posey had a humorous as well as a poetic sense and turned the former to advantage in a series of letters written by an imagined Creek named Fus Fixico, who committed to writing all his front-porch ruminations and conversations with his neighbors. The resulting correspondence was published in several Indian Territory papers, including the Eufala *Indian Journal,* which Posey himself edited. When, for instance, Posey listed all the resources of Indian Territory that might be sent to the exposition in St. Louis, he carefully noted that along with oil from "Bootlesville" (Bartlesville) and cotton from Eufala, one should send some "hot air from Checotah."[24] Although the principal object of Fus Fixico's attention was the Creek government and especially its chief, Pleasant Porter, who used a finely tuned patronage system and his power to countersign the deeds by which Creeks were given their allotments to manipulate individuals who were otherwise uncooperative, Anglos were also the object of Fus Fixico's jibes. Those involved in the politics of allotment he often characterized with a humiliating name: Judge Stew It (Stewart), Rob It Owing (Robert Owen), Damn Big Pie (Tams Bixby), Senator It's Cocked (Hitchcock), and President Rooster Feather (Roosevelt). The convention to draft a constitution for the Indian state of Sequoyah is described as underrepresented because they "didn't had that many lawyers that could dig up they car fare and settle the hotel bill and blow theyselves for a morning's morning in Shawnee." Rising from a riot of derelicts "all bend over their beer kegs," one speaker received an ovation for his efforts equal to "when William Ginning Bryan hoodooed the Democrats in Chicago," while another speaker is described as "a Cherokee, but I think he was druther be a Republican."[25] It is unfortunate that these letters have not been collected and published, because they belong squarely in the tradition of frontier humor exemplified by Mark Twain, Artemus Ward, and Josh Billings and bear no little resemblance to the dialect ethnic humor of someone like Peter Finley Dunne's Mr. Dooley. A man of many talents, Posey must have understood what his humor was doing to the image of the stoic Indian; he frequently published under the pen name of Chinubbie Harjo, the Creek Trickster figure.

Another Indian Territory writer, John Milton Oskison, a Cherokee born in Vinita in 1874, was different in every way from Posey. He left the Territory for an education at Stanford, where in his senior year, 1898, he won

Century magazine's short-story competition for "Only the Master Shall Praise" (59 [1900]:327–50). This prize story, with its themes of cowboy loyalty, pride in range skills, and exaltation of the "code of the west," shows no interest in Indian life but rather seems to have drawn attention as a result of the popularity of writers like Owen Wister. The same is true of other Oskison stories, including "When the Grass Grew Long," "The Quality of Mercy," and "Young Henry and the Old Man," which however skillfully accomplished seem all style, pleasing but insubstantial.[26] Indeed, despite his later newspaper and magazine editorials on Indian issues, Oskison was more widely known as a writer of frontier romance (see chapter 4).

Charles Eastman, the Santee Sioux physician whose autobiographical works made him a celebrity in the first decades of this century, was also a writer of popular fiction. His stories mined the same vein he first opened in *Indian Boyhood* (1902), and it was undoubtedly the success of this work that prompted him to collect some of these sketches and tales, which he had successfully placed in magazines like *Harper's* and *Ladies' Home Journal*, into *Red Hunters and Animal People* (1904), which he followed with *Old Indian Days* (1907) and *Smoky Day's Wigwam Evenings* (1909), all published by major eastern houses.

Some of these stories are Kiplingesque animal fables. "The Great Cat's Nursery," although not a tale of great significance, is an impressive exercise in which Eastman sustains the entire narrative through the point of view of a puma mother who in the end gives her life defending her cub. In "The Grey Chieftain," about two Indian hunters seeking bighorn sheep, Eastman dramatizes the intimate relationship of knowledge, respect, and communication between hunter and hunted. "War Maiden of the Sioux," a brief sketch that originally appeared in *Ladies' Home Journal* (August 1906), tells of Makatah, who accompanied a war party to avenge the death of her brothers at the hands of the Crows. Many of her suitors flee the battle, and she returns to shame them by announcing herself the widow of the man who stayed and saved her life, winning her heart and the battle. The virtue of these stories is less artistic than polemical. Eastman used his fiction to illustrate that the cultural perspectives brought by Native Americans to roles Anglo Americans had taken for granted were not only novel but morally sound, practical, and valuable.

Another Sioux writer, Zitkala-Ša (Red Bird) was born on the Yankton Reservation in 1875. After a traditional upbringing she left at age twelve for the Quaker Indian School in Wabash, Indiana. When she came home she found herself alienated from her family and community. She returned to school, completing her higher education at Earlham College, and after graduation taught at Carlisle. She married an Indian agent, Raymond Bonnin, and worked for many years on Indian reservations in the West. She joined the Society of American Indians and became a lifelong advocate of assimilation, including allotment, citizenship, and abolition of the BIA. In 1922 she founded the National Congress of American Indians and lobbied Indian causes in Washington, especially the Citizenship Bill of 1924. She died at age sixty-one, after a long career in public life.[27]

"The Trial Path" (*Harper's,* October 1901, 741–44) is a conventional story of traditional Indian life, in which the primary attraction of the narrative is the conjunction of novel Siouan customs and the interests of conventional romance. The same is not true for "The Soft-Hearted Sioux" (*Harper's,* March 1901, 505–8), a five-part narrative distinguished by its keen dramatization of the alienation created by acculturative processes like those Zitkala-Ša experienced in Wabash. A sixteen-year-old Sioux youth whom all thought destined to be a hunter and warrior is instead sent off to mission school for "nine winters where I hunted for the soft heart of Christ." When he returns he finds he is unable to provide for the needs of his dying father or disabuse him of his faith in the medicine man. In fact, so poorly does his new Christianity meet the exigencies of reservation life that he is compelled, in a rigidly deterministic way, to engage in the very things he had learned to detest: hunting, killing, even murder. And because he can no longer provide for those who depend on him, the tragedy has social as well as individual consequences. By tale's end we see that it is not the "cunning magician," as an apparent agent of the devil, who defeats the efforts of the Christian, but the self-destructiveness of the Christian's own acculturative program.

The principal long work of this period is *Queen of the Woods,* a novel by Simon Pokagon, published in 1899, a year after his death. Born in 1830 the son of the Potowatomi chief who signed the Treaty of Tippecanoe (1826) and also sold the area that became Chicago to the whites, Simon was sent away to spend three years at Notre Dame preparatory school and to complete his college education of Oberlin. He spent most of the remainder of his life trying to secure just compensation for the sale of Chicago; although he collected $39,000 after visiting President Abraham Lincoln, he continued to press his people's claims until a settlement of $104,000 was made in 1896. He was considered the "best-educated full-blood Indian of his time" and became known as the Indian Longfellow.[28]

Queen of the Woods is a disturbing combination of autobiography and apocalyptic. When young Simon, while hunting, first sees Lonidaw, the future "queen of the woods," she is accompanied by a white deer wearing a red, white, and blue wreath. The deer pines away as Lonidaw becomes enamored of Simon. Simon and Lonidaw eventually marry and raise two children, Olondaw and Hazeleye. The boy Olondaw is sent away to school reluctantly, for his mother had dreamed of meeting a snake in the path that ate two little robins, one of which was transformed into Olondaw. Vision becomes prophecy when the boy returns home an alcoholic and perishes shortly thereafter. Hazeleye's canoe is overturned after being struck by the boat of a drunken fisherman, and Lonidaw plunges in after her, but cannot save her daughter from drowning. She later dies of pneumonia contracted that fateful day. The tale culminates with Simon's promise to Lonidaw to fight for temperance, and there follows an apocalyptic vision of King Alcohol, robed in the Stars and Stripes, out of which come snakes and ravens to stalk the land in a terrible parody of John Gast's popular 1872 painting, *American Progress*. The annihilation is complete when Indians begin to die of spontaneous combustion.

By almost any standards Pokagon's novel is a very awkward construction, but because of his education it is impossible to attribute that awkwardness to ignorance of literary form. If anything, his knowledge of the Bible's apocalyptic tradition and of conventions of symbolization urged him to strive for a grander presentation of theme than he was capable of satisfactorily achieving. Examined constructively, the difference in diction and form between the final apocalyptic section and the idyllic earlier portions may reflect Pokagon's desire to portray a shift to a larger-than-individual stage—fable or myth, for instance—where he can assign historical causality and moral responsibility. Then the parodic figure of King Alcohol, merging as it does the historical aspirations, biblical justifications, and technological innovations of America's Manifest Destiny, becomes potent with irony and tragedy, catching up motifs Pokagon has scattered throughout the book: the snake who consumes the robins; the "firewater" breath of Olondaw; the white deer with the bunting wreath; the priest who sends the boy to school, where he becomes a drunk; the white sport fisherman whose drunkenness causes two deaths. Against this awesome darkness, we recall the idyllic sun-dappled existence of the Queen of the Woods and are compelled by the fabulous melodrama to take some measure of the great loss.

In this period, which saw the emergence of a written Native American literature in English, most native writers preferred nonfictional genres to communicate the impact of invasion, warfare, and displacement. But as the historical, autobiographical, and ethnographic traditions began to flourish, the outlines of a distinctive Native American poetry and fiction were also emerging, portending a literature of power and beauty that would emerge into fullness in the twentieth century.

Chapter Four
Modern Fiction

Reaction and Reform

With the implementation of the Dawes Allotment Act (1887), most Americans came to adopt attitudes toward "the Indian problem" that one historian has charitably described as "unproductive."[1] For the moment the consciences of once-active reformers were relieved of their burden of guilt, for the act dangled before them the hope of Indian self-sufficiency and affirmed their comfortable beliefs in individualism, capitalism, and assimilation. Without Indians in the headlines, the same reservation conditions that had prompted reform encouraged both the cynic and the romantic to believe that Indians were "a vanishing race," a myth that ironically was becoming popular in the East just as the Indian population was recovering. In western states, where Indians were visibly present, the act whetted the appetites of private citizens and of state and local governments for Indian land and resources.

The beginning of this century also saw the emergence of "Red Progressive" Indian leaders. Their Society of American Indians (SAI), which included the writers Gertrude Bonnin, John Oskison, and Charles Eastman, promoted a pan-Indian perspective and opposed the paternalism of the Bureau of Indian Affairs (BIA), advocating instead a self-help policy. They generally endorsed assimilationist means if not ends, however, and ignored the issue of freedom of religion to gain political support by opposing the Peyote religion. Attempts to eradicate the Peyote religion were only part of a larger, reactionary BIA program to suppress tribal religion entirely. After World War I, reformers mobilized around John Collier and former SAI members to oppose this aim, as well as the government's unilateral opening of executive order reservations to oil developers and the Bursum Bill, an outrageous ploy to award New Mexico Pueblo lands to white squatters by requiring tribes to establish clear title back to the Spanish period. After the Bursum Bill was defeated and some housecleaning had taken place at the BIA, reformers successfully lobbied Congress to extend citizenship to all Native Americans in 1924. Until then it had been conferred upon only a small percentage in exchange for taking allotments or serving in World War I (15,000 Indians enlisted), although it was not until 1948 that Arizona and New Mexico became the last states to remove obstacles to the free exercise of voting rights. A series of government inquiries culminated in the explosive Meriam Report (1928), which found, among other things, that in the face of general and infant mortality rates two and three times as high as for the white population, the government had been spending only fifty cents per year on the health care of each of these new citizens.

Roosevelt's election in 1932 inaugurated a New Deal for Indians. Collier was named Commissioner of Indian Affairs and strove to reform old policies in the direction of self-determination and ethnic pluralism. The principal accomplishment of the New Deal was the Wheeler-Howard or Indian Reorganization Act (IRA) of 1934. It permitted tribes to organize their own governments under constitutions of their own devising; ended allotment and restored surplus land to the communal land base; established Indian-preference hiring in the BIA; and provided funds to underwrite loans to tribal businesses, to purchase land to add to tribal land bases, and to support Indian students. In keeping with the principle of self-determination the law applied only to those tribes who voted to accept it. Of the 189 tribes that endorsed it, 135 later established tribal governments. The act was rejected by seventy-seven tribes for reasons ranging from distrust of the federal government and personal animosity toward Collier to cultural resistance toward the possible forms of self-government. A mixed success, the IRA nevertheless marked a watershed in federal Indian policy. Native writers who had suffered the consequences of allotment and assimilationist policy began to count the cost, and some, including D'Arcy McNickle, who joined the BIA, actively promoted the Collier reforms. Against this background of continued unrest, Native American authors increasingly sought new creative outlets.

Modern Fiction

Native writers of frontier romance. The infant girl born in 1888 in Idaho and baptized Christal Quintasket was given the Indian name Hum-ishu-ma or Mourning Dove. According to Dexter Fisher, Mourning Dove's "paternal grandfather had been an Irishman who worked for Hudson's Bay Company and who apparently had married her Indian grandmother under false pretenses."[2] Mourning Dove was raised by the grandmother with knowledge of both her tribal heritage and this family past; both emerge in her novel. Her education was scanty—a short period in Catholic and government schools, some training in typing and English at a business school—but in 1914 she entered into a collaboration with Lucullus McWhorter, a Washington State historian and author, allowing him to edit and annotate her novel in manuscript. *Cogewea, the Half-Blood,* finally appeared in 1927. As Fisher amply illustrates, McWhorter's principal effect upon the novel was to confuse the narrative voice by intruding overblown language and to burden an otherwise straightforward narrative with expositions on Indian history and tirades against government incompetence and white venality.

At its heart the novel is a simple romance, cut from the stock of early western writers like Owen Wister and Emerson Hough. Having been raised by her Indian grandmother, the Stemteema, after her Irish father abandoned her to join in the Alaska gold rush, Cogewea returned from Carlisle Indian School to work on the Idaho ranch of her brother-in-law, John Carter. An attractive woman, she is eagerly sought after by Jim LaGrinder, another half-blood, and Alfred Densmore, an eastern tenderfoot hired on a whim to help out with the upcoming roundup. Cogewea is joined for the summer by her Stemteema and her younger sister, who try to dissuade her from encouraging a relationship with Densmore, whom we discover later has a fiancée back east and is only out to gain what he believes is Cogewea's fortune. She evades the Stemteema's disapproval by eloping with Densmore, but once out of town Densmore discovers that she is not wealthy at all and robs her of the savings she had withdrawn to finance their elopement. He escapes and is never caught, but Cogewea, chastened by her experience with whites and moved by Jim's devoted attention, finally marries the right man. She is further rewarded when a complication in her father's will leaves her a quarter of a million dollars of his Alaskan gold fortune, instead of the twenty dollars he had originally intended.

The novel is more typical of the popular romantic fiction current in 1914, the year of its conception, than in 1927, the year of its publication. Its flaws are those of most popular fiction. The naive young girl, noble Jim LaGrinder, craven Alfred Densmore, and the Charlie Russell cowboys are all types, and the inevitability of the marriage to Jim is so clear that her prolonged relationship with Densmore is incomprehensible. Yet the novel is important, and not simply because it is the first novel written by a Native American woman. Despite its many artistic failures, the commonness of its plot is made strange, endowed with larger significance, because the domestic melodrama has been infused with the burdens of the historical tragedy. In the literature of the age of Allotment and incompetency hearings, the marriage compact had replaced the treaty, and was treated by Anglos with the same lack of respect.

John Milton Oskison (Cherokee) had all the advantages that Hum-ishuma lacked.[3] From his college days he was a successful short-story writer (see chapter 3) and had even won several magazine prizes. In the first decade of this century he wrote editorials for *Nation* and later went to work for *Collier's* and the *New York Post*. During the same period he became an active member of the Society of American Indians, and many of his published editorials took up Indian causes. In the mid-1920s he turned to writing novels, for which the Indian Territory of his youth provided the setting. Unfortunately, his novels, like his short stories, are mass-market fiction at best, and offer little insight into Indian life or concerns.

The first of his novels, *Wild Harvest* (1925), is a frontier romance between Tom Winger and Nan Forest, complicated by rival suitors, a tempting seductress, murders, and bank robberies. In the end, however, we know that Tom and Nan, like Cogewea and Jim, will marry. Indian characters have only minor parts, as they do in all of Oskison's fiction, although the action is set in the Allotment era, and both Tom and Nan argue in favor of allotment and assimilationist goals. His second novel, *Black Jack Davey* (1926), is another romance, this time between Davey Dawes and Mary Keene. Dawes and other white settlers move onto alloted land in Oklahoma, their principal opposition coming from Jerry Boyd, who married a Cherokee woman in order to own land in her name. Boyd tries to eliminate Ned Warrior, from whom the Daweses lease their land, but in a showdown scene it is Boyd who is killed. *Brothers Three* (1935), in many ways a familiar Depression novel, concerns the three Odell brothers, who are one-sixteenth Cherokee and have grown up on their father's ranch in Indian Territory. Timmy, the eldest, becomes a small businessman in the nearby town, storekeeping and running an automobile agency. After mismanaging a cattle business, then losing the family fortune in a bad mining investment, Roger becomes drunk and ends up paralyzed as a result of an auto accident. Henry moves to New York and, following the pattern of Oskison's own life, becomes a writer. On the stock market he recoups Roger's loss and more, but subsequently loses it all in the Crash. In the end, May, the part-Cherokee wife convinces the family to return to Odell land and work to build it back up.

Although Oskison's writing is much more accomplished than Mourning Dove's, both writers were bound by their experience of popular fiction, its stock characters and stereotyped expressions. If Mourning Dove was a far less skilled writer than Oskison, she at least struggled to make her unromantic life compatible with the demands of romantic fiction. Oskison, on the other hand, carefully drew up situations and figures that did not deviate from the conventions of the genre, and consequently relegated the issue of Indian life to the background.

John Joseph Mathews. Born on November 16, 1894, his name was inscribed on the tribal roll in 1906 as one-eighth Osage. Throughout his life Mathews was acutely aware of being a mixed-blood, set apart from the more traditional full-blood Osages by his "progressive" upbringing. His University of Oklahoma education was interrupted during World War I for European service as a flight instructor, but he returned to take a degree in geology in 1920. In that year, too, he refused a Rhodes scholarship to enter Oxford's Merton College, where he earned a bachelor's degree in natural science in 1923. After a period of travel, he returned home to Pawhuska, Oklahoma, in 1929, where he completed *Wah'Kon-tah: The Osage and the White Man's Road* in a little less than five months. A Book-of-the-Month Club success, it embarked Mathews on a writing career through the 1930s and 1940s, while he also served on the Osage Tribal Council. Besides other volumes of history and autobiography, he published one novel, *Sundown* (1934), and, according to Terry Wilson, at his death in 1979 he left completed manuscripts for another novel and a two-volume autobiography.[4]

Although Mathews said of *Sundown* that he "sat down and wrote it [and] never read it since it was published," the novel has been more difficult for others to put aside.[5] The story is set at the turn of the century in Osage country, where oil leases are already accruing profits to those who can make the system work for them, and where unspoken distances separate full- and mixed-blood Osages. Into this world is born Chal Windzer, named by his progressive father, who hopes that he will be "a challenge to the disinheritors of his people" (4). But Chal is a deeply divided character from the start, internalizing both his father's progressive orientation and his full-blood mother's attraction to the land and distrust of whites. As a youth he desires the approval of girls he comes to despise and envies the assertiveness and apparent integrity of full-blood boys who occasionally bully him.

As much as family, education is a momentous force in Chal's life. At reservation school he is patronized by an eastern teacher trying to recover her belief in Fenimore Cooper Indians she knows do not exist anymore. From the reservation, he goes off to college accompanied by two of his full-blood friends, Running Elk and Sun-on-His-Wings. All three have been recruited for their football prowess (this is the age of Jim Thorpe), but patronizing attitudes and demands for conformity drive his friends back to the reservation. When his own desire to be accepted, even by those he despises for their "obvious insincerities," leads him to accept a humiliating paddling as part of his fraternity's pledge court ritual, he masks his abiding anger with a smile. Later he transfers that anger to the team's quarterback, when, lined up behind him during practice, he imagines a knife slicing the back of his neck. When Running Elk refuses to be paddled, he earns from Chal a comparison to a noble bull buffalo, facing down a pack of wolves. But the comparison highlights the depth of Chal's ambivalence, for he condemns himself in admiring the integrity of his full-blood friends. When they drop out of the university, he is relieved to be free from associating with people "so backward" (112). At bottom, this "vicarious shame" (68) he feels for full-blood friends who do not seem to want to join the white man's world is displaced self-hatred, for he is plagued with unaccountable desires to run, to strip down and dance or swim, to sing at the top of his voice, which he identifies as an almost genetic Indianness and tries to suppress.

These internal divisions make mature relationships impossible for him. At college he meets Blossom Daubeny, a campus queen, and spends long periods daydreaming of ways to change himself into a white image of success, a businessman or an "elegant man of the world" (153), anything but an Osage. He curses himself to sleep, wishing that "I didn't have a God damn' drop of Indian blood in me" (160). After joining the Army Air Corps when World War I breaks out, he meets Lou Kerry, a married white woman whose attentions flatter him, and before whom he abandons all self-esteem by approving of her presumptuous identification of him as Spanish; he even wishes he could add a title of royalty.

Chal returns home after the war unmotivated, inactive, alienated from the traditionalists and small-town life, yet not caught up in the progressive frenzy for material success. Throughout the last half of *Sundown,* Mathews uses the ebb and flow of derricks across the prairie to mark the progress of indolence and vice associated with the Osage oil boom. Freed from the obligation to work when he inherits $25,000 on his father's death, Chal joins the Oklahoma version of the Lost Generation careening in convertibles through the blackjacks.

Attempts to get in touch with the life of the tribal community by attending dances stir him inwardly but do not alter his behavior. His first understanding of what is happening to him comes during a religious ceremony when he hears Watching Eagle's speech on the consequences of following the white man's road, a speech dramatically prefaced by the announcement of the murder of Running Elk, who of late had become addicted to drugs and alcohol.[6] Although Chal returns from the speech to his life of indolence, forces are building within him. He abandons a drinking bash with his friends, driving his car across country at high speed. Stopping in the middle of a field, he gets out to dance, "to challenge something; to strut before the enemy." Although this act of assertiveness cannot break through the "dammed up emotion," he realizes what he cannot express: "that he was a glorious male . . . a brother to the wind, the lightning and the forces that came out of the earth" (297).

When the oil boom collapses and the white models of success have committed suicide and their Osage counterparts stalk the streets as paupers, a Senate committee arrives to investigate the Osage oil murders. The highlight of the hearing is Roan Horse's very brief speech: "You have come here twenty-five years too late" (306). Although he had characterized Roan Horse as an "insurgent," one who "believed that everything was wrong," Chal feels proud after hearing his speech and joins others who "in some vague way, [felt] that Roan Horse had been their champion" (307). He returns home, angry at his mother because she seems unaware that something important, which he never explicitly identifies, is happening in the world. As the novel ends, she challenges him about his future plans. He responds that he will become an orator and go to Harvard Law School, an idea that fills him with "an assurance and courage he hadn't felt for years" (311), and he falls asleep on the front porch, confident he has met his mother's challenge.

It is difficult, even for sympathetic readers, to be optimistic about Chal's future. Things happen to him too quickly, accompanied by too little apparent interior change, for readers to consider his law school plans anything more than another evasion of reality. "The ending of *Sundown* resolves nothing," Charles Larson writes, but this is too harsh a judgment.[7] Many of the elements of Watching Eagle's speech echo sentiments we know are Chal's. He is also dramatically moved by Roan Horse's speech, which likewise capsulizes his experience and gives shape and meaning to his past, so that he understands his story as but one episode in the larger history of his people. This is the insight that rouses his anger against his mother, who "didn't seem to be aware that something important had happened to the little world of their blackjacks and prairie" (308). Although he may not become a lawyer, we can at least understand why the idea is not only an appealing but an honorable desire for him.

Sundown is only a partial artistic success. It is occasionally overwritten, a failing that always tempted Mathews, and its pace can grow tiresome. As a consequence the novel is initially unsatisfying, lacking any kind of obvious climax to anchor an episodic structure and sacrificing plot almost entirely to characterization. But in Chal Windzer Mathews presents the first thoroughly developed example of a character who will become all too familiar, described frequently but mistakenly as "caught between two worlds." In fact his condition is less a suspension between two sets of values than a confusion of both at a single moment. Paralyzed, he endures but hardly seems to change. Inarticulate, he expresses himself only in occasional spasms of violent action. Alienated, he seeks solace in drink and a sense of community in the company of the cynical and despairing. In clarity if not intensity of vision, *Sundown* equals D'Arcy McNickle's *The Surrounded,* although the latter surpasses it artistically.

   D'Arcy McNickle.   D'Arcy McNickle was born in St. Ignatius, Montana, January 18, 1904, on the Flathead Reservation, a member of the Confederated Salish and Kutenai Tribes. Graduation from the University of Montana in 1925—an education he financed by selling his land under the Allotment Act—was followed by a year at Oxford and later a summer at Grenoble. After a stint at writing in New York, he joined the Bureau of Indian Affairs in 1936 as assistant to the commissioner, John Collier, abetting the latter's efforts to reverse assimilationist federal policies. Later he cofounded the National Congress of American Indians and served as the first director of the Newberry Library's Center for the History of the American Indian. As an administrator, historian, or professional anthropologist, his first concern was Indians, especially the issue of tribalism, maintaining the multiplicity of distinctive traditional cultures, which gives the lie to all stereotypes and resists the forces of assimilation. When he died in 1977, he had published many volumes of history and anthropology, some specifically on this topic, but perhaps none of his writings spoke as passionately and as effectively as his first, a novel published in 1936, *The Surrounded.*[8]

   With artful economy, McNickle unfolds the story of Archilde Leon, who returns from government school (Chemewa) in Oregon to his (Flathead) reservation. The valley in which the reservation is located, McNickle's epigraph tells us, is called "*Sniel-emen* (mountains of the surrounded) because there they had been set upon and destroyed." The novel extends this more historical meaning of the name to the contemporary struggle to escape the oppressive confinement of Christianity, of patronizing and incompetent federal bureaucrats, of arbitrary enforcement of alien laws, and of exploitation by white entrepreneurs. Agents in the valley community make sure no one goes unwatched, and game wardens and county sheriffs ride the ridges to guarantee that no one from below escapes.

We are led to expect that, like Chal Windzer, with whom he shares educational opportunities and the approbation of "progressive" elements, Archilde ought to be able to challenge this environment. Max Leon, his Spanish father, believes that, unlike his six other sons, Archilde might be able to make something of himself. Fr. Grepilloux, the aging Jesuit missionary, associates Archilde with Big Paul, a figure from the past who was killed trying to reconcile Indians and whites. Convinced that "Big Paul should also have had his victory, and might have had it if he had come later," the priest hopes that the era of waiting is over, that education and Christianity have effectually combined to replace the collapse of the old life, and that "this boy might be the promise of a new day—" (97). Together they plan a future for Archilde, who has developed some moderate musical skill at school, entrusting him first to a local priest with a talent for music and then dreaming of sending him to Europe. But realizing these dreams, which emanate from two men cut off from the realities of reservation life, is impossible for Archilde, who is slowly drawn back into the agony of his community.

Underlying Archilde's story is that of his mother, Catherine Running Wolf. In the mid-nineteenth century, her father had welcomed the Jesuit missionaries into the valley. She herself had become such a devoted convert that she had been known as "Faithful Catherine." But her marriage to Max Leon introduced her to the consequences of living in a world of white men who never changed their place of residence; who lived by the clock, not by the sun; who turned away relatives from the door; who, in short, were all that she was not. Increasingly embittered, Catherine struck back by implicating Max in a cattle-rustling scheme that was really the sole work of their first son, and during the trial deliberately refused to speak English and exculpate her husband. Max narrowly avoided conviction, but the distance between them had since grown so great that she began living a more traditional life in a cabin while he, according to his customs, slept in the frame house, the two only communicating through intermediaries.

When Archilde returns, he discovers that his brother, Louis, has been stealing horses and hiding out in the mountains returning only to visit his wife, Agnes, and his children, Mike and Narcisse, or to get food. As summer passes Archilde makes little progress toward penetrating the silence that separates him from Max and his mother. With fall approaching, Catherine persuades Archilde to take her hunting, fearing she may never get up to the mountains again. In the mountains they encounter Louis, who has killed a small doe. When a game warden shoots Louis while trying to arrest him for poaching, Catherine releases her accumulated anger in a single instinctive stroke by plunging a hatchet into his skull. For "Faithful Catherine" it is an unpardonable sin. Believing on the one hand that God will not forgive so heinous an act, and accepting on the other hand a dream that shows her isolated in a heaven populated only by whites, she abandons her Christianity and returns to the Salish practice of public confession and whipping. Later, as she lies on her deathbed, she insists to Archilde that she wants no priest. When a young priest arrives nonetheless, Archilde, although not yet strong enough to dismiss him summarily, lets him go to his mother only because he comprehends the futility of the priest's actions.

After drawing suspicion upon himself by covering up for his mother's actions, Archilde responds to the urgings of Elise LaRose, an embarrassingly assertive boarding school runaway whom he finds attractive, and flees to the mountains with her and Louis's boys. Sheriff Quigley, a figure whose silent menace has stalked the whole book, suddenly appears out of the woods, intent on arresting them. Fearing nothing, desiring everything, Elise shoots him, hoping to be free at last, but the Indian Agent and Indian Police appear and arrest them. The young boys flee, but Archilde and Elise are handcuffed as Agent Parker remarks: "It's too damn bad you people never learn that you can't run away. It's pathetic—" (297).

Although the ominous Sheriff Quigley approaches stereotype, there are no monochromatic characters in this novel. Kind Fr. Grepilloux, after a long and sympathetic exposition to Max of the injustices suffered by the Indians, adds "what in his heart seemed to balance all that he had set against it—'they had God' " (59). The agent, Parker, "liked his job and he liked his Indian wards. He saw their helplessness and realized, without getting excited about it, that he was of little use to them. He did what he could but he was hampered by a system which penalized initiative and by the Indians' own poor understanding of what was expected of them . . . in a word it was a nightmare" (151, 152). Even the venal trader Moser, who had hoped to make an easy fortune buying land through allotment sales, understood that "the justice of the procedure was . . . a question if you looked closely" (30). And Max, for all his sullenness toward Catherine, can at least get enough distance to rage at Moser that people are "freezing to death in those shacks by the church. They don't know why; they had nothing to do with it. You and me and Father Grepilloux were the ones brought it on. For what good?" (147). Most of the characters find themselves trapped in a life of compromise, victimized by the system they perpetuate or coopted by the system they oppose. The Indians are not the only surrounded.

But McNickle illustrates painfully the walls erected by assimilationist education. Archilde returns to the dusty valley despising the changeless character of the place and considers refusing an invitation to a feast because, as he describes it, "you gorged yourself on meat until you felt sick, and a lot of old people told tiresome stories" (4). Louis returns from the mission school brutal, sullen, foul-mouthed, disrespectful of his parents, charged with a barely repressed violence and a hatred of authority; he becomes a thief. And young Mike returns from the same place, a bedwetter plagued by nightmares.

For the surrounded, the only victory is a private one, the interior peace and solidarity that come with returning to tribal values. In this process Modeste the elder plays a pivotal role, using stories to impress upon all attending the validity of the traditional perspective. Hearing Modeste, Archilde understands his people's past for the first time because "he had really seen it happen" (74). Mike is restored too by serving blind Modeste as a guide. Although the Fourth of July celebration in which they dance has become secularized, even assumed a carnival atmosphere, they dance with dignity and authority, refusing to be burdened by circumstance. For Archilde, this, finally, is the message of his mother's "repaganization."

But McNickle is not hopeful. Despite the undercurrents of New Deal reform beginning to swell in his time, his novel is grimly deterministic. However much Archilde's inarticulate urgings, like Chal's, point the way, they never resolve the internal divisions that separate even him and Elise: "they were as far apart as worlds bobbing along side by side. They ached to rush through their intervening world shells, but it was always not quite—reach and surge as he would, and press up to him as she would. Always not quite . . ." (290). The imposition of an alien perspective has permanently intruded upon him a self-consciousness that precludes the peace of total surrender he identifies with "paganism." Absolute integrity of vision is no longer possible. Experience is refracted through multiple lenses and cannot be made to focus.

From Termination to Self-Determination

Many of the more than 25,000 Native American veterans of World War II did not remain on the reservations after their tour of duty ended, but returned to cities where they joined a growing urban Indian population attracted by wartime economic opportunities.[9] At the same time, the federal government responded to the burden of public debt incurred during the war and to the clamor of postwar growth by adopting policies to "terminate" the federal-Indian trust relationship, effectively freeing the timber, water, mineral, and energy resources for private developers. After a long period under New Deal principles of self-determination, the country's mood, especially in western states, turned against "overprivileged" Indians, as one politician described them, and sounded again the call for expropriative assimilation.

During the 1950s, Congress and the Secretary of the Interior both rode under the spur of Senator Arthur Watkins (R.-Utah), the principal advocate of Termination. Watkins and others pressured the Secretary of the Interior to remove restrictions on sale of Indian lands, which eventually cost Indian peoples the loss of 4.1 million acres. Congress also authorized several states to extend criminal and civil jurisdiction over Indian reservations. And in 1953, House Concurrent Resolution 108 directed that the federal status of several tribes be terminated immediately; during the course of the next ten years sixty-one Indian groups lost their federal status. Tribes were not allowed to vote on the specifics of the termination plan designed for them, only on the concept of exchanging land and federal status for a cash award. As a concept, termination was especially attractive to many urban Indians who did not depend on the reservation, but who could share in the award as enrolled members of the tribe. In practice, however, Termination proved a disaster. In exchange for valuable timber land, for instance, every Klamath person received $50,000, which disappeared as fast as the land had. The Menomini found their reservation converted into a Wisconsin county and exhausted their financial benefits trying to create or maintain services previously provided by the federal government. Throughout the mid-1960s, Congress tried to extort termination plans from tribes in exchange for further federal actions such as dam building (Seneca) or settling claims (Colville).

A key element of the termination policy was the relocation program, designed to encourage migration to the cities. Begun in 1952, it provided "vocational training, travel money, moving expenses, and assistance in finding jobs and housing, in addition to one year of medical care and a month's subsistence allowance."[10] But vocational training did not always suit the job market and, in an alien environment, no real support systems were in place to sustain a sense of community and identity. About 30 percent of the 35,000 Indians relocated to Los Angeles, Seattle, Chicago, and other cities returned to their reservation homes. Nevertheless, by the end of the 1960s nearly one-third of the country's 1 million Indians lived in cities; by 1980 the urban Indian population neared half a million.

The 1960s and 1970s, like the 1930s before them, were an era of investigation and reform, accompanied by visible Indian activism. President Johnson included Native Americans in his Great Society legislation, and President Nixon, in a 1970 Special Message to Congress, reiterated and strengthened Johnson's commitment of the federal government to "self-determination without termination." Congress also repealed the Menomini termination legislation, restoring the tribe to federal status with its own land. Native American novelists like Momaday and Silko captured the inner realities of displacement from the land and cultural alienation resulting from wartime experiences, relocation, and urbanization and offered hope of renewal.

Contemporary Fiction

N. Scott Momaday.   Momaday was born on February 27, 1934, in Lawton, Oklahoma, the son of Alfred M. Momaday, a Kiowa artist of the traditional style, and Natachee Scott. His early memories of life in the house and arbor near Rainy Mountain, Oklahoma, his family's move to Hobbs, New Mexico, during World War II, and their settling down afterwards in Jemez Pueblo have been set out in his poetic autobiography, *The Names* (1976), one of his most experimental and intricately textured pieces of writing. He received a Ph.D. from Stanford (1963) in comparative literature and is currently teaching at the University of Arizona. In 1969 he was awarded the Pulitzer Prize for his novel *House Made of Dawn* (1968).[11]

Although it is more European in form and style and more urban in setting than any other Native American novel, Momaday framed his work with the traditional Jemez formula words for "opening" *(Dypaloh)* and "closing" *(Qtsedaba)* a story, thus claiming for his tale the power of tribal myth to pattern experience. The Prologue is an anticipation of the final scene and turns the novel into a complex, four-part flashback.

Part 1, "The Longhair," is set at Walatowa (Jemez) during the late summer of 1945 and comprises six sections, each covering selected events for a specific day. Francisco hurries from his fields to meet his son, Abel, returning home from World War II; the youth stumbles off the bus into his arms, drunk. Also introduced are Father Olguin, the resident priest, and Angela Grace Martin St. John, a wealthy doctor's wife, up from Los Angeles for her health. Abel answers her inquiry for someone to split firewood; her physical attraction to him contrasts strongly with her alienation from the land and her own body. During a chicken pull, part of the feast of Santiago, the patron saint of the pueblo, Abel appears for the first time out of uniform. His efforts to reenter the life of the community through this event, however, are checked by his own awkwardness and by an albino who, having skillfully plucked the rooster from the ground, pins Abel against a wall and humiliatingly beats him with the bloody rooster. That night, Fr. Olguin takes comfort from the seventy-five-year-old journal of Fray Nicolas, which illustrates its author's self-deception, self-righteousness, and presumption. Abel comes to realize that as much as he desired "to enter into the old rhythm of the tongue . . . he was no longer attuned to it. [He was] not dumb—silence was the older and better part of custom still—but *inarticulate*" (57). His alienation is highlighted during lovemaking with Angela, when he holds her apart briefly at the last moment as much to deprive her as to assert himself. The climactic events of part 1 occur on August 1, the feast of Porcingula. Francisco remembers the gravity and the difficulty of assuming the role of the bull who chases boys pretending to be Spanish invaders during the feast, of being "a kind of victim, an object of ridicule and hatred" (75). After the feast, Abel confronts the albino and kills him. The next day he flees.

Part 2, "The Priest of the Sun," opens six years later with an image of grunion cast upon a California beach, vulnerable and out of their element in the moment of their continuance, and shifts immediately to the Los Angeles basement church of John Big Bluff Tosomah, urban Indian trickster, peyote roadman, and focus of a community of relocated Indians including Abel and his Navajo friend, Ben Benally. The first section is divided into two parts, beginning with Tosomah's homily on St. John's gospel, "In the beginning was the Word . . . ." The second consists of Abel's memories as he lies on a cliff near the ocean, following a second brutal beating by the sadistic cop Martinez; memories of the grunion; peyote services; his trial, where Fr. Olguin had argued that Abel had killed what he thought was a witch; the kindness of Milly, the social worker who befriended him. Foreshadowing the end, he sees Indians running "in the way of least resistance, no resistance . . . with great dignity and calm, not in hope of anything, but hopelessly; neither in fear nor hatred nor despair of evil, but simply in recognition and with respect. Evil was. Evil was abroad in the night; they must venture out to the confrontation; they must reckon dues and divide the world" (96). For Abel, who had "wandered to the end of the earth, was even now reeling on the edge of the world" (96), this vision and the memory of the grunion provide him with the perspective necessary to reshape his sense of himself and his future. The last section is an adaptation of Momaday's introduction to another of his works, *The Way to Rainy Mountain*. But here the words take on more urgency, rooted in the anger of

Tosomah's acknowledgment that having to make this journey to recover his past is a measure of the degree of his displacement from it. The "vision of deicide" and the Kiowa disaster at Palo Duro Canyon become sources not just of mourning but of rage, and Tosomah confesses to Benally that at times he dreams of "a full red moon, a hunter's moon, and a . . . wagon train full of women and children" (136).

The third part, "The Night Chanter," narrated by Benally after Abel has left to return home, focuses on the problems of Abel's adjustments to the city and the inability of the Relocation program to compensate for important emotional and spiritual losses so that Indians can successfully manage the transition to wage work and urban life. Instead, they struggle to find some sense of self and community in alcohol and late-night powwows on a hill above the city, despairing the American Dream that lured them. Benally is himself a deeply divided character, who has compromised his expectations by settling for a menial job and tenement housing, while idealizing reservation life. Abel cannot keep a job or manage his relationships with Benally and Milly, but drinks more and more, becomes sullen, and expresses himself only through outbursts of rage. To keep Abel going, Benally shares with him a dream of getting together back on the reservation at a later time, of putting the bottle away for good, of riding fine horses up into the mountains to sing old songs, but one senses that Benally, who has committed himself to city life, needs this dream even more than Abel. After Martinez the cop cracks Abel's outstretched hands with a nightstick for not paying off during the shakedown, Abel vows to get even, but he regains consciousness after the confrontation to discover his hands broken, his body wrecked. Shortly after being discharged from the hospital, he takes the train home.

Part 4, "The Dawn Runner," opens by contrasting Fr. Olguin, withdrawn within the dead Fray Nicholas's journals, and Abel, attending to his dying grandfather, who for the past six days has been mumbling words that make no sense to Abel. On this last night, however, Francisco recounts memories that heal Abel, touching as they do upon relations with women, the land, whites, his community, and climaxed by the memory of running the race, begun "at a better man's pace" that had quickly brought agony. But "the moment passed, and the next and the next, and he was running still . . ." (187–88). Before dawn Francisco dies, and Abel ceremonially prepares his grandfather's body for burial. He wakes Fr. Olguin, demands that he bury Francisco, and turns away abruptly. Then, after first stopping to daub his body with ashes from an oven near the edge of the village, he joins the runners racing for rain and fertility in the new year.

As a dawn rain begins to fall, washing the ashes from his body, he recalls Benally's "House Made of Dawn" prayer from the Night Chant: "There was no sound, and he had no voice; he had only the words of a song. And he went running on the rise of the song" (191).

The most enigmatic figure in the novel is the albino, who is not pure symbol, having, as Fray Nicolas's journal tells us, historical precedents in the community. But the albino certainly represents the impersonal, malicious force of white power felt as prejudicial fate. His serpent like qualities clearly align him with Martinez, the *culebra* or snake. But there is more. The albino's death is shrouded in allusions to Christ's, but their value is inverted because they are not associated with Abel, for whom we care, but with his antagonist. At the moment of his death, the albino embraced Abel "in benediction" and "drew him in close, and the terrible strength of his hands was brought to bear only in proportion as Abel resisted them" (78). Larry Evers has provided the most subtle reading of the albino, suggesting that, because he is Indian, killing him is Abel's way of freeing himself from all those forces he has internalized, which, like "the white immensity of flesh [which] lay over and smothered him" (78), stripped him of his pride, immobilized his will, and prevented him from reentering the community.[12] Following this line of thought, the "proportional strength" of the albino would assume two dimensions. Socially and historically it suggests that white efforts to dominate Indian peoples increase in the face of resistance—probably, given the albino's embrace, because such resistance is perceived by whites as personal rejection. Individually and interiorly, it requires of Abel a redirection of his energies (which he does not accomplish until the end of the novel) from a destructive, other-focused struggle to a creative, self-directed growth, "running in the path of least resistance."

The words and song rising in his heart as he runs toward the dawn signal the beginning of Abel's regeneration. Although as yet he has no voice, he is no longer inarticulate, having found both words and the appropriate rhythm. The power of language is one of Momaday's most enduring themes. He identifies with Tosomah in believing that "only in language can a man realize himself complete." That Abel's slide toward oblivion has been reversed in these last moments becomes clear the more one hears Momaday talk about language: "An Indian is an idea which a given man has of himself. And it is a moral idea, for it accounts for the way in which he reacts to other men and to the world in general. And that idea, in order to be realized completely, has to be expressed. . . . There is no way we can live apart from the morality of a verbal dimension."[13]

Leslie Marmon Silko.   Leslie Silko was born of mixed Laguna, Mexican, and Anglo ancestry in 1948, the great-granddaughter of a trader, Robert Gunn Marmon, who, like his brother Walter, became an important figure in Laguna Pueblo, where he settled, even to being elected to a term as its governor. Very much aware that, despite these events, her family held a marginal position in the community—even attaching significance to the fact that their house was on the edge of the village—she quickly became conscious of how the "stories," a term embracing everything from gossip and not-so-ancient history to myths, bind a community together, providing it and each member with a distinct identity. Silko earned a B.A. in English from the University of New Mexico in 1969. In 1981 she was awarded a prestigious MacArthur Fellowship in recognition of her achievement in fiction and poetry. [14]

Silko's novel *Ceremony* (1977), like Momaday's, is about a World War II veteran. Tayo returns to Laguna Pueblo from combat in the Pacific via a veterans' hospital in southern California, unrelieved of an enormous burden of guilt. When he had enlisted with his cousin Rocky, on whom the hopes of the family had been placed and with whom he had been raised, he had assumed responsibility for him, but Rocky had died in his arms while being marched to a Japanese prison camp. Then Tayo had cursed the jungle rain; now he returned to find the land in a drought for which he felt culpable. He had also left his uncle Josiah with the entire task of managing a new herd of Mexican spotted cattle for a chance to look down his rifle barrel at faces that resembled his uncle, who he returns to find has died in his absence. And throughout his youth his Christian aunt had made him feel ashamed for his mixed blood and for having to live with them because of his mother's promiscuous past.

The war provided only the catalytic shock necessary to galvanize the forces working to alienate him from his land, his family, his tribe and tradition, even from his own flesh. More corrosive than the war had been Auntie's Christianity, which "separated people from themselves; it tried to crush the single clan name, encouraging each person to stand alone, because Jesus Christ would save only the individual soul" (70). [15] Home-economics teachers taught girls to dress "exactly like the white girls" (71), while the science teacher "explained exactly what superstition was, and then held the science textbook up for the clans to see the true source of explanation" (99). All it took was the experience of total war, especially its final, atomic destruction, to convince Tayo that for tribal elders the white world was "too alien to comprehend" (38).

The experience almost destroyed Tayo, as it had others who returned, including Emo, Pinkie, and Harley. He no longer had a usable past; his "memories were tangled with the present . . . as he tried to pull them apart and rewind them into their places, they snagged and tangled even more" (6). He experiences bodily dissociation, becoming "invisible scattered smoke" and merging "with the walls and the ceiling, shimmering white, remote from everything" (14, 33). When the doctors interview him before his discharge, he responds by referring to himself in the third person (15). He is close to becoming a witch like Emo and others who, having lost touch with their own deadened bodies (137), suffer a devitalized sexuality (175) and curse the earth (25). Although Tayo tries to deceive himself by observing "how easy it [was] to stay alive now that he didn't care" (40), Ku'oosh and the elders know that being human requires both energy and responsibility, and they point out to Tayo that it only takes "one person to tear away the delicate strands of the web, spilling the rays of the sun, and the fragile world will be injured" (36). A ceremony is required to reintegrate Tayo's self by reimpressing upon his fragmented psyche the whole mythic pattern of the culture hero and his quest, thus restoring the shape of his personal and communal history and reestablishing his identity.

Because their own traditional ceremony for contact with dead enemies does not heal Tayo, the elders send him to Betonie, an unconventional Navajo medicine man distrusted by most traditionalists because he uses phone books and other paraphernalia gathered in his travels as part of his ceremonies. He argues that the ceremonies have been changing from the beginning, and must grow if they are to meet present needs: "There are balances and harmonies always shifting, always necessary to maintain. . . . It is a matter of transitions, you see; the changing, the becoming must be cared for closely" (137). Because the visible present is only the historical dimension of a mythic struggle between the death-seeking forces of witchery and the nurturing powers of life, vigilance is required. Witchery has been astir from the beginning, searching for rents in the web of meaning in order to gain entry into the present moment. Betonie's Mexican grandmother, Descheeny's wife, emphasized that this struggle is universal and eternal, by sending him off to school, because the conflict is "carried on in all languages now" (128).

Silko mobilizes the potential of this dualism to focus the mythic struggle embodied in the conflict between Tayo and Emo through her plot's central metaphor of ceremony. Navajo ceremonialism, on which Silko bases her plot, requires *myth*, which sets the pattern for the event, *rites*, which reenact the prototypical events, and *medicines,* which effect the integration of the prototypical and the historic. Since ceremonies were taught to The People by mythic heroes who had themselves been the first patients of their patron supernatural beings, the Holy People, the roles of *patient* and *patron/ medicine man* are functionally convertible. Silko provides the mythic base for Tayo's story by incorporating the independent Laguna myths of Arrowboy and the Gambler, as well as the Navajo myths of Coyote Transformation and Cub Boy, into the myth of Earth Woman's flight and Hummingbird's quest to bring her back. Set against this is the antimyth of the origins of witchery in the shamans' contest, epitomized in Emo's antistory of identity loss and subhuman sexuality (59–61). Betonie extends the Hoop, Sandpainting, and Bear's Den rituals central to the mythic ceremony, into Tayo's life, sending him on a search for a woman, the spotted cattle, a mountain, and a constellation of stars. Emo consummates the antiritual by torturing Harley in a manner identical to the witches' meeting; Pinkie's metallic pounding on the truck hood replaces the heartbeat of a drum in a ceremony of death whose final sandpainting is the blast pattern of an atomic explosion. Antithetical to the traditional life-giving medicines of pollen and water are the destructive poisons of uranium and alcohol. Where Pa'cya'nyi and the Ck'oy'o witch are respectively the first victim and patron of the seductions of witchery and the models of those like Emo who live on the dying of others, it is the Earth Woman/Yellow Woman figures—Descheeny's wife, Night Swan, and Ts'eh—who are working for rain, healing, fertility, and Tayo's restoration.

The novel rewards what Silko calls "the ear for story and the eye for pattern"[16] by inviting the reader to explore ways in which Tayo's story converges with the underlying mythic structure. Leaving Betonie to search for the spotted cattle, Tayo meets Ts'eh, a member of the Montaña family, who lives on Mt. Taylor (Tse-pina), the Laguna sacred mountain, with her brother. She may in fact be a mountain spirit and he a Mountain Lion Man. Her blue shawl links her with both Descheeny's wife three generations earlier and Night Swan, with her blue sheets and dress, women who are themselves related to Tayo and Betonie by their hazel eyes and Mexican ancestry. All three are associated with rain and a vital sexuality. Silko emphasizes the healing function of Tayo's making love to Ts'eh by polarizing the values associated with water; she contrasts the lovemaking (188), likened to the sudden, gentle collapse of a bank into warm river water, with an earlier, terrifying incident when Tayo thought he would sink into a urine- and water-flooded floor when a toilet backs up in a bar's bathroom (58). Like Betonie, Ts'eh becomes a vehicle for self-conscious storytelling, informing Tayo that witchery has its own, violent endings to stories, including this one. Mythic and narrative time (201) and space (248) converge as the climactic confrontation approaches. At the scene of Harley's torture, Tayo resists the urge to rush to Harley's rescue and kill Emo, because he knows that to savor the power of hatred and death is to surrender to witchery. Instead, confident from his experience with Ts'eh that larger powers are at work keeping order, Tayo lets the motion of the stars carry the world and himself through this moment. When Harley and Leroy's pickup crashes, when Emo kills Pinkie and flees to California, Tayo knows that witchery has rebounded upon itself. As the elders had hoped, his purification and healing provide for the renewal of his community and the continuance of its life despite the wounds of the present generation.

By creating a narrative structure that, like Tayo's consciousness, integrates an initially fragmented presentation into a coherent, linear narrative, Silko transforms not just Tayo's story but her narrator's telling into a ceremonial event, framed by sunrise prayers and motivated by the assertion that she is telling us the story that Thought-Woman, the Creator, is thinking. Because of the convertibility of the roles of patient and medicine man mentioned earlier, the novel implies that several such stories and ceremonies are embedded within it. In the end, Tayo's story, through the agency of the narrator, becomes for us our ceremony of reading and, in restoring some of our shared humanity despite our cultural differences, offers us a healing equal to Tayo's.

The power of the mythic perspective to shape our experience of the world is also at the heart of Silko's short fiction, which she has collected with her poetry in *Storyteller* (1980). The title story is about an Eskimo woman who shares her hut with an old man who makes passes at her when he is not mumbling a story about a polar bear that has turned to stalk the hunter pursuing it. Anxious for other company, she flirts with local whites, but is brought to disgust when a sexual encounter turns into a nightmare and to hatred when she learns that the local trader had poisoned her parents. She exploits the man's lust by leading him out onto thin ice, where he drowns in the river. In "Yellow Woman" a young Laguna woman meets a Navajo down by the river while she is getting water; when he addresses her as Yellow Woman, she begins to wonder whether she is indeed living out a myth in latter times, and he, of course, does nothing to disabuse her of the ideas. Witchery is central to "Tony's Story," which, like Simon Ortiz's "The Killing of the State Cop" and perhaps the trial scene from *House Made of Dawn,* is based on the actual murder of a policeman by two Acoma youths who perceived him to be a witch. [17] Silko's achievement lies in realizing more fully than any of her contemporaries the possibilities of Native American myths and the storytelling frame, not just for ethnographic "local color" or even for a context of allusion, but for providing the vital principle for plot construction and characterization.

James Welch.   James Welch was born in Browning, Montana, on November 18, 1940, of Blackfeet descent on his mother's side, Gros Ventre on his father's. After attending schools on Fort Belknap (Gros Ventre and Assiniboine) Reservation and the Blackfeet Reservation, he moved for a time to Minneapolis, where he graduated from high school and attended the University of Minnesota for a year. He returned to Montana to earn a bachelor's degree from the University of Montana. In 1971 he published a collection of poetry, *Riding the Earthboy 40,* and followed this with two novels, *Winter in the Blood* (1974) and *The Death of Jim Loney* (1979).[18]

As the title suggests, the nameless narrator of *Winter in the Blood* suffers from acute alienation. After a second operation on his bad knee, he has returned from a hospital in Tacoma to a desolate High Plains landscape populated by familiar strangers: "Not one of them meant anything to me. And for no reason, I felt no hatred, no love, no guilt, no conscience, nothing but a distance. . . . The country had created a distance as deep as it was empty" (2). His mother, Theresa, is distinguished by her assertiveness, her assimilationist hatred for Indians (although she herself is Indian), and her demoralizing comments. In a small but typical show of power, she recalls to him that it was she, and not his father, who had killed Amos, the pet duck of his childhood, and served him as Thanksgiving turkey. His father, First Raise, had frozen to death in a snowdrift returning from a drinking spree, but the narrator remembers him with affection as a dreamer, someone good with his hands, who liked to make people laugh and who loved his sons. Theresa fills his place with Lame Bull, who calculated that he "had married 360 acres of hay land, all irrigated, levelled some of the best land in the valley, as well as a 2000-acre grazing lease" (13) and who always refers to the thirty-two-year-old narrator as a "boy." The other permanent resident is his grandmother, feeble and nearly blind, who rocks away her days, when not eating mush or smoking, contemplating killing the narrator's girlfriend, Agnes, with a knife she keeps in her legging. The girl is a young Cree (traditional enemy of his grandmother's Blackfeet people) who fantasizes through movie magazines; before the narrator returns, she absconds with his rifle and razor.

The narrator sets out on several trips to nearby towns, supposedly to recover her and his things. The trips are distinguished by two kinds of encounters. The first is the almost absurdist drama involving white males like "the airplane man," who insists through his discontinuous monologues (one can hardly call them "conversations") that he is being chased by the FBI and needs the narrator's help to cross over into Canada. After a series of deadpan visual jokes—an old man dying face down in a bowl of oatmeal, the narrator hiding behind the purple teddy bear he is carrying—the insanity is made dangerously real when the airplane man is in fact arrested by the FBI amid sirens, whirling red lights, and a gathering crowd. The second are encounters with women who bring him back to their places for the night. After he wakes up one morning and enters the woman's "cocoon-like" bedroom to try to touch her, she freezes his hand and his passions with the twice-repeated command, "Beat it!"—whereupon he leaves. In a moment of oblique vision he sees in another woman with whom he has spent the night all the dominating women in his life, and when she asks him for oral sex, he slaps her brutally but unemotionally. Finally, an important memory is triggered by passing an old movie poster of Randolph Scott "grinning cruelly" (103). He remembers how his brother Mose had been killed one evening while the two of them were trying to hurry some cattle across a highway. An old cow had balked at the gate to the range of the far side, stalling the herd on the highway. Just as Bird, the narrator's horse, broke instinctively after a calf who had raced away from the bunch, the narrator caught a glimpse of a car hurtling past him, heard the impact, and saw his brother's body fly over the vehicle.

He returns home to find everyone making arrangements for the burial of his grandmother, who has died in his absence. As he saddles Bird for a ride out to visit Yellow Calf, an old Indian living in the hills who had told him that the deer had warned him "the world is cockeyed" (69), he absolves the horse of guilt for its part in Mose's death and acknowledges his own. Yellow Calf illuminates the story of his grandmother's marriage to Standing Bear, the famed Blackfeet chief, which he already knew, adding that after misfortune struck the tribe it was blamed on her, and she was abandoned by the other women, who had always been envious of her beauty. And the narrator discovers that through the bitter winter that followed, it had been Yellow Calf who had provided for her, hunted for her, loved her, and that he, and not a mixed-blood drifter named Doagie, was his real grandfather. He rides back to the ranch in a cleansing rainstorm only to find a wild-eyed cow mired in the sticky mud of a slough and dying from exhaustion. Unable to throw a loop around the animal's neck, he wades in to fasten the rope and lead her out. But Bird collapses and dies in the struggle to pull her out, the cow slips back forever into the mud, and the narrator crawls out totally spent, lying in the rain. The novel closes with the grandmother's burial, highlighted by a sardonic eulogy by Lame Bull. Throughout the narrator remarks on the break in the harsh weather, thinks of fishing again, and casually observes that he might take up his relationship with Agnes on a more serious note. The ceremony and the book close when the narrator throws his grandmother's tobacco pouch into the grave.

Despite the black humor, the austere language, and an ending of sufficient ambiguity to cause difficulties in interpretation, *Winter in the Blood* is a hopeful book. In the mock-epic struggle to rescue the mired cow, there are signs of a recovery of commitment to life to replace the internalized distance. Against natural inclination (187) and in spite of the burden of guilt and shame they bear from prior experience, both the aged horse and the alienated narrator plunge into a consuming struggle to save the beast. The cow itself brings back memories not only of the "wild-eyed spinster" responsible for the death of the narrator's brother (166), but is associated with all those women who have so caustically unmanned him throughout the novel, of all forces, in fact, that have conspired to turn him into a "servant to the memory of death" (38). There is no reason to make more of this than a small show of commitment, especially in view of the narrator's persistently distanced point of view in the burial scene. No great and sudden reversals are promised here. But in his attention to the breaking weather, which reminds him of his homeward journey from discovering that Yellow Calf is his grandfather, in his returning the tobacco pouch to his grandmother as a mark of respect and a token of connection with the past, and in his casual but not irrelevant thoughts about his Cree girl friend, there is a hint of a thaw.

One does not have to read very far into Welch's second novel, *The Death of Jim Loney,* to foresee for its title figure a less optimistic prognosis. In a small Montana town whose only distinction is that it was the home of the 1959 Class B High School Basketball champions, a team of which he was a member, Jim Loney suffers from an enduring inability to engage life. Abandoned by both his parents—Ike, a white transient who returned to take up residence in a trailer outside town, and Eletra Calf-Looking, who left Ike to marry the father of George Yellow Eyes—Loney feels no attachment to either or to their respective cultures.

His girl friend, Rhea, a white schoolteacher who moved up from Dallas, tries to nurse him through his disaffection and his drinking. In his dreams and drunken stupors he often sees the image of a dark bird hypnotically hovering and calling to him. He dreams of meeting a woman in a graveyard who is looking for her lost son; Loney volunteers to help the woman find him. After all of this Rhea wants to take him to Seattle to start anew, but Loney is unaccountably tied to this particular landscape. When Rhea's efforts fail, she endorses the plan of Loney's sister, Kate, a prominent Washington, D.C., attorney, to take him back to that city and set him up there, but when Kate returns for that purpose she also fails to move him.

Instead Loney wanders on to meet Myron Pretty Weasel, one of his former championship teammates, who takes him out hunting. On the hunt both think they see a bear, an unusual occurrence in those parts, and split up to track it. In the midst of a reverie about George Yellow Eyes, Loney suddenly "heard the brittle crashing of the dry stalks and he saw the darkness of it, its immense darkness in that dazzling day, and he thrust the gun to his cheek and he felt the recoil and he saw the astonished look on Pretty Weasel's face as he stumbled two steps back and sat down in the crackling cattails" (120). Loney assumes guilt for what appears on the surface to be a hunting accident, perhaps because in that "immense darkness" he saw the emptiness of his own life heightened by the substantiality of the lives of Yellow Eyes and Pretty Weasel, lives that could have been his future if he had not been abandoned by his mother.

He returns to town to visit Rhea and to try to get some perspective on himself from his father, to whom he has not spoken in years. With him he leaves word where he is going, knowing that the police will interpret this as a desire to be caught, perhaps even killed. As he waits for the end in the mountains, Loney's last thoughts turn to the dream about the mother in the graveyard looking for her son. He longs for "another place where people bought each other drinks and talked quietly about their past, their mistakes and their small triumphs; a place where those pasts merged into one and everything was all right and it was like everything was beginning again without a past. No lost sons, no mothers searching. There had to be that place, but it was not on this earth" (175). When his pursuers locate him in Mission Canyon, a site believed by local Indians to be a portal into the next life, he steps out from behind his cover, permitting himself to be shot. As he falls, the last thing he sees are "the beating wings of a dark bird as it climbed to a distant place" (179).

Although marked by the same concern for style and texture, this novel is less satisfying than his first. From beginning to end, what we are allowed to know about Loney provides no aesthetically satisfying reason for his death, and although we can be assured he is relieved by it, we are not. While it is clear that none of Loney's relationships is meaningful, it is not clear that the possibility of meaning is itself foreclosed. Rhea and Kate, it is true, are cut from the same emasculating mold as Welch's other women, the first a smothering mother replacement, the second an intimidating competitor. It is also true that there are no traditional figures like Yellow Calf who could provide the knowledge necessary for a change in direction. Yet it is also clear that, in their own way, Ike, Myron Pretty Weasel, even the miserably brow-beaten Clancy, although all wrought from the same environment as Loney, have made a separate peace with the world that enables them to carry on. Full of dark hints and glimmers of foreboding, the novel only suggests and does not reveal the motivation that finally moves Loney from depression and drunkenness to despair and suicide.

Nevertheless, despite the bleakness of circumstance in both novels, Welch's narrative voice speaks of a great and intimate love for both the land and the people about which he writes. If he writes of pain, it is because he has known its wound; of humor, because he knows its curative power. Because he cares so deeply for the craft of his telling, we know through his clean, deceptively simple prose the depth of his care for those like Loney whom he must watch plummet to their transfiguration.

Other novels and novelists.   A flurry of Native American novels were published during the 1970s, several of which merit discussion because they represent new directions in form or theme for Native American fiction.

In 1978 D'Arcy McNickle's *Wind From an Enemy Sky* was published posthumously.[19] It reflects many of the same interests that occupied McNickle in his first novel, *The Surrounded* (1936), but most of the characters in the present work are placeholders in a moral struggle whose abstract outlines are only too visible. Bull, the aging traditionalist, lacks Modeste's power deal with the whites; instead he adopts an isolationist position. His brother, Henry Jim, has alienated himself from Bull and precipitated a growing factionalism by successfully taking up wheat farming and adopting other white customs, by becoming Christian, and by surrendering the Feather Boy medicine bundle to a priest who had it sent away to a museum. This already difficult situation is complicated by the recent completion of a government dam in a high mountain cirque, a tribal sacred site. The diverted water, originally intended for Indian allotments in the hot valley, was instead being used by whites, who had purchased the allotments rejected by Indians who preferred traditional life in the cooler foothill camps. When Bull returns from seeing the dam, which he had never believed to exist—"How can a stream out of the mountains be killed?" he asks (14)—he defends Pock Face, a young hothead who had killed a dam worker. The slain worker is the nephew of Adam Pell, the dam's designer and an eastern liberal whose college contacts with a Peruvian Indian had excited him about the possibilities of doing something about "the Indian problem." Pell, it turns out, also owns the museum to which the priest had sent the Feather Boy bundle. He assumes full responsibility for the dam, which now insults and deprives the people it was commissioned, at least overtly, to serve, and for the medicine bundle, which has been misplaced and has rotted away from carelessness. In suggesting he will return the medicine bundle, however, he misleads several people, including the conscientious superintendent and Henry Jim, who by this time has died after mending his fallout with his brother by taking up traditional ways. When he arrives, he compounds the error of his misrepresentation by insisting on offering as "compensation," a monetarily valuable but spiritually worthless gold Incan figurine of a naked woman. Bull's accumulated anger flares suddenly, and he shoots Pell and the superintendent before allowing himself to be killed by the tribal policeman.

Although McNickle's focus on water rights and sacred places makes this novel very contemporary, in form and theme much of it seems dated. Bull's violence in defense of tribal values, however, is meant to be a real alternative to the passive determinism of *The Surrounded*. This entire novel constitutes a cynical reply to the ineptness and impotence of "reforming" forces McNickle had served in the Bureau, and their failure to displace tribalism, the heart of Indian life as he saw it, that which Archilde called in the first novel "paganism" and which is emphasized here by Henry Jim's deathbed rejection of white values and customs.

The contemporary emphasis on native religious perspectives in Native American fiction is highlighted by the work of Hyemeyohsts Storm, a Cheyenne born in Lame Deer, Montana, in 1935. Storm published his first novel, *Seven Arrows* (1972), amid a great deal of controversy.[20] Set in the mid-nineteenth century, it recounts the decline of the Sun Dance religion and the Brotherhood of the Shields, which had united the Plains nations. It is comprised of several chain stories linking principal Cheyenne, Crow, and Sioux figures through time from the Massacre at Sand Creek (1864) to the anticipated, but never narrated, engagement with Custer at the Greasy Grass (Little Bighorn) in 1876. The historical story is complemented by the efforts of several medicine people to enlighten their friends about the Way of the Shields and of Seven Arrows, the Culture Hero. The stories they tell, Storm informs us, are meant to be read as elaborate allegories. Unfortunately, Storm has one character explicate that which another narrates, while yet a third voice provides a historical dimension. The burden of this intensely self-conscious, affected mode of presentation shows up clearly when contrasted with the graceful, suggestive presentation of mythic perspective in Silko's *Ceremony*. In his second novel, *The Song of Heyoehkah* (1981), the girl Estchimah is on a vision quest to become a shamaness. Her story is interpolated with the story of three Indian survivors of the Plains Wars and three white goldseekers. The whole comprises a sequel of sorts to the first book.

In trying to effect an accommodation between a native point of view and a non-native audience, *Seven Arrows* runs a number of risks, most of which are also assumed in the second work. The visuals in both books, especially the shields in the first, do not derive from traditional Cheyenne designs but reflect a colorful and impressionistic mystic personalism. Combined with the romantic Curtis photographs of the first book and the assumption, implicit in the first and explicit in the second book, that its white audience is spiritually hungry for Cheyenne religion, the final effect suggests an attempt to exploit a particular segment of the youth culture.

A very different sort of novel is *Darkness in Saint Louis Bearheart*, by the Anishinabe (Chippewa) writer Gerald Vizenor (1978).[21] Vizenor, born in Minneapolis in 1934, took his B.A. from the University of Minnesota in 1960 and did graduate work there as well. The novel's plot consists of what appear at first to be unrelated episodes. During the takeover of the BIA offices in Washington, a young woman who belongs to the radical American Indian Movement (AIM) finds a manuscript written by a bureaucrat named Saint Louis Bearheart; this manuscript composes the bulk of Vizenor's novel. It is a dark vision of a future time when the government, having felt the crunch of oil shortages, directs the cutting of forest preserves, including a stand of sacred cedars guarded for generations by the Cedarfair family, most recently by Proude Cedarfair. To avoid a confrontation, Proude and his wife, Rosina, take to the road, and in the course of their journey enlist in their pilgrim company a number of fantastic characters, many of whom Vizenor anticipated in his collection of sketches called *Wordarrows*.[22] These include members of a commune of women poets who live in a "scapehouse of weirds and sensitives" (31); a small man with a huge penis he has named President Jackson; a homosexual tribal lawyer and his lover, the tribal historian, Wilde Coxswain; and many others. The names of the characters alone would suggest the novel's debt to the European picaresque tradition, but certain of the episodes point to the tale's roots in Native American tradition. Many of the characters are Trickster figures, for instance, and in the pilgrims first encounter with Sir Cecil Staples, who gambles their lives for gasoline that he controls, we see a contemporary realization of the story of the Evil Gambler, whose defeat restored life and rain. Vizenor also creates original fables from the psychology of contemporary America, such as the death of Little Big Mouse, a white woman who surrendered herself to cripples in sympathy only to be torn apart by their lust for wholeness.

In calling this a postmodern novel, Alan Velie drew attention to essential features of style, especially its pointed juxtapositions of disparate realities, its heavy reliance upon sex and violence as metaphors for meaninglessness, and its deliberate challenge to conventions of form and decorum. But the novel is not all aesthetic "play," "devoid of philosophical and artistic depth."[23] In accommodating, however imperfectly, Trickster cycles to written literature (as Silko did with culture-hero myths), Vizenor adopted not only the content but the form of oral tradition. But he went a step further. At the end of the novel, Proude and a companion arrive at Chaco Canyon, New Mexico, where they pass through a window in the Anasazi ruin of Pueblo Bonito and, changing into bears, float "into the fourth world" through the rising winter-solstice sun. Thus he gives focus and meaning to the picaresque journey that dominates the reader's consciousness with an emergence story having strong culture-hero–transformational themes. It is a mode of transcendence that portends a new beginning and a way out of the confinement and confusion, so painful and yet so laughable, that dominate this world in the imagination of Saint Louis Bearheart. It offers a powerful counterpoint not only to the desperate strategies of the young AIM girl who is supposedly reading this manuscript but to the reader who has been peeking over her shoulder. A lot of the novel is, as Velie suggests, "bad art," with much strained allegory and facile humor, but this is nevertheless an important book, not so much for what it achieves as for the tremendous possibilities to which it points.

Chapter Five
Contemporary Poetry

In 1969 N. Scott Momaday was awarded the Pulitzer Prize for *House Made of Dawn*, a novel that featured a Native American protagonist stymied into inarticulateness by his brutal confrontation with Anglo culture. Ironically, in the same year, a special issue of the *South Dakota Review*, "The American Indian Speaks," first brought to public attention a number of today's principal Native American poets, a profusion of voices: visionary, conversational, incantatory, narrative.

Several of the poets in that anthology first discovered their gifts as writing students of T. D. Allen at the Institute of American Indian Arts in Sante Fe. From its beginnings the IAIA had ventured into English-language poetry as a field of artistic endeavor for its students as legitimate as sculpture, painting, or dance. Allen encouraged her students to draw upon traditional poetic forms and emphasized the need for strong visual images that would communicate powerfully and immediately the dimensions of personal experience. Following a pattern set by Lloyd Henri New's Phoenix Indian School anthology *The New Trail* (1943), she had the best of these works published in a volume entitled *The Whispering Wind: Poems by Young American Indians* (1972). The success of this program encouraged Allen and the BIA to expand the program to other Indian schools. The results of this second effort were four privately printed volumes that were subsequently gathered into a single collection called *Arrows Four* (1974). In that year, too, many of the IAIA poets appeared in Dodge and Mc-Cullough's *Voices from Wah'Kon-tah*. Writing continues at the IAIA, bearing visible fruit through their publication *Spawning the Medicine River*. Today a number of presses and publications regularly feature Native American poetry, especially *Blue Cloud Quarterly, Sun Tracks, Strawberry Press,* and the *Greenfield Review*. Both Harper & Row and Viking have supported major publishing efforts in this area.

For many decades following Pauline Johnson's pre–World War I success, native poets were not widely published. The American taste for "Indian Poetry" was really a cultivated one, part of the wave of exoticism that swept literary circles in the 1920s. Anglo poets were not exempt from this mood. In the pages of *Poetry, Dial,* and *Nation,* Mary Austin, Eda Lou

Walton, Alice Corbin Henderson, and others persuaded many of a conflu-
ence of aesthetic interest between Native American poetry, as recorded by
ethnographers like Frances Densmore, and the Imagist movement of
Pound and H.D. and the populist movement of Sandburg and Lindsay.
For the longest period Anglo writers like Austin and Lew Sarrett offered
"interpretations" of native poetry, much in the manner of today's "ethno-
poets" and "white shamans"—for example, Jerome Rothenberg, James
Koller, and Gary Snyder. They not only preempted any audience an original native poetry might have found; their derivative forms set the public
taste for a certain kind of "Indian Poetry."

The only native poet then being published, Lynn Riggs (Cherokee), did
not identify himself as an "Indian" poet or with this movement, but con-
centrated on mastering his craft. Riggs, today best known for his play
Green Grow the Lilacs (the basis for the popular musical comedy *Oklahoma!*)
published a few poems in the pages of *Poetry*, almost academic exercises in
elevated diction and traditional rhymed forms. In 1930 Riggs collected his
poems into a volume he titled *The Iron Dish* (Garden City, N.Y.: Doubleday, Doran). Although some of these are stuffy and overblown pieces (e.g.,
"Portrait of a Peer" and "Pilgrimage: The Gargantuan Flight") he was able
in poems like "Still Season" to move with a simple grace. A skilled versifier
he occasionally created very impressive moments, like this one where
rhymes, sprung by heavily stressed syllables, click into place:

> Surely we may be no bitterer
> Than the shrunk grape
> Clinging to the wasted stem
> It cannot escape.
>
> (43)

Riggs was an imagist, poetic heir to the impressionists. The second stanza
of "A Letter," written in New Mexico:

> In my neighbor's garden chickens, like snow,
> Drift in the alfalfa. Bees are humming;
> A pink dress, a blue wagon in the road;
> Guitars are strumming.
>
> (11)

The "Santa Domingo Corn Dance" is a series of nine such pictures organized dramatically, the first entitled "The Chorus" and others "Dancers,"

"Koshari," and so on up to the last stanza, "Rain." Drama, in fact, was the medium for Riggs's successful career.

As Riggs's example indicates, Native American poetry cannot be stereotyped. The groupings that follow are merely points of departure. As usual, it is more rewarding to attend to personal vision and emerging individual style than to any generalizations.

The Formalists

Although all poets are concerned with language, these poets seem more conscious of the variety of stylistic resources available to them, perhaps because as a group they are familiar with American and European literary traditions and not infrequently seek models there. Many hold advanced degrees and teach literature professionally. They share a preoccupation with the external form of the poem, an often deliberately convoluted syntax, and distinctive gifts for metaphor and verbal irony. Two of them, Momaday and Rose, explicitly seek their emerging identities in their craft.

N. Scott Momaday (Kiowa) won the Pulitzer Prize for fiction in 1969 with his novel *House Made of Dawn.* Readers of the novel who recall the impassioned statement of Tosomah on the power of the word will not find it surprising that its author is also a poet whose concern for language marks his every line. Momaday's own position resembles Tosomah's: "I have a great deal of respect for the beauty of language, and I believe that only in language can man realize himself complete."[1] Although his first book of poetry, *Angle of Geese,* was not published until 1974, the earliest dated poem in the volume is from June 1960. A second volume *The Gourd Dancer* (1976), incorporated the first and added as many new poems. The sum of his achievement is most noticeable in several cycles of poems. The cycle form gives him the opportunity to develop a theme through modulations of voice and imagery while retaining a lyric intensity. Two are particularly effective.

"Plainview" is a cycle of four poems. The ambiguous title may refer to a particular place, as in Plainview, Texas, or more generally to a view (meaning not only "scene" but "sense") of the Plains, or even to assumptions about perception and the act of seeing. The last two are more to the point. The heroic couplets of "Plainview: 1" endow the speaker's personal vision with epic dimensionality; the onset of the storm disrupts the almost hallucinatory presence of eleven magpies, an odd, disquieting number, standing motionless on the plain, challenging our willingness to believe that what we see is real. In "Plainview: 2" the heroic couplets are exchanged for the rhythms and refrains of Navajo song and the image of an old Indian drinking and dreaming of a blue-black horse. The song of the horse comes to dominate his consciousness until the scene begins to capture in epitome the loss of vitality Momaday attributes to the passing of the horse culture. "Plainview: 3" is a brief image of the sun rising over the prairie, casting its fire across the plain, driving back the night; it is an image that reecurs in "Rainy Mountain Cemetery," an image of the dawning of a new era. In "Plainview: 4" the poet remembers visiting the abandoned house of Poor Buffalo, who married the Kiowa captive Milly Durgan, taken from Texas as a child. (Momaday's great-grandmother Keahdinekeah was also a Mexican captive from Texas.) His voice, adopting the ballad form of "The Texian Boys," a brief quotation of which opens the poem, is answered antiphonally and finally by the chorus of another Anglo folksong: "And we'll rally round the canebrake and shoot the buffalo." In that instant the memory of popular culture merges with the eradication of a symbolic animal, a people, and a way of life. This is the disquietingly plain view of a land that speaks.

In the cycle of four poems that compose "The Gourd Dancer," Momaday harmoniously unites the themes of land, history, memory, family, and race. The first poem, "The Omen," assumes the presence of the engaged imagination before the house of his grandfather Mammedaty, built on Kiowa land near Rainy Mountain, Oklahoma: "Another season centers on this place. Like blood the memory congeals in it." In the dark epiphany of an owl, a bird associated with death, rising into the trees, Momaday recognizes the presence of the past. The second poem, "The Dream," presents Mammedaty as a man of dreams whose life responds to the impress of existence rhythmically as the alternation between sound and silence, between drumbeat and interval in a dance. The third section, "The Dance," is Momaday's most complex metrical form, a six-line stanza, the first of which is a single trochaic foot; the second through sixth lines are composed of two, three, four, four, and five iambic feet, miming the outward spiraling pattern of the dance. In the fourth and final poem, "The Giveaway," Momaday interrupts the motion of the dance to have young Mammedaty's name announced. In this naming ceremony, he is presented with a beautiful black horse, and in the augmentative rhythms of catalog, elevating prose to poetry, we sense the boy's deepening wonder before the animal: "the horse wheeled and threw its head and cut its eyes in a wild way. And it blew hard and quivered in its hide so that the light ran, rippling, upon its shoulders and its flanks—and then it stood still and was calm."[2] In

"The Gourd Dancer" all of Momaday's poetic gifts are orchestrated into dazzling art.

Besides being a graphic artist of reputation whose distinctive illustrations grace several books, Wendy Rose (Hopi/Miwok) is a mature poet. Her first book, *Hopi Roadrunner Dancing* (1973), demonstrated that she possessed from the beginning a real gift for stunning visual imagery that she combined with a flare for wordplay and an unwillingness to compromise with painful realities. In this yoking of the potentially romantic with the brutally realistic, her poetry found its first source of strength. Her second volume, *Long Division: A Tribal History* (1976), is a slim chapbook of a dozen poems, but poem for poem, it is her best work and reveals the steady progress of her craft. The long lines of these poems show much more control than her initial efforts, a newly developed ear for aural effects, and an emerging skill in playing the visual against the aural through the use of good enjambments loaded with spring and suspense. The latter are especially noticeable in the title poem: "the reverse snap of a leaf at / thirty-below, the jump / from tree to tree covered in squirrel fur," and ". . . and some part / of this world, old and pagan, just / holds on."[3] In these poems, too, the formal diction is often in counterpoint with the sarcastic tone ("O we are / the natives") or the brutal image ("It's our blood that gives you those / southwestern skies").[4]

Academic Squaw (1977) was motivated by the ironies inherent in being both an anthropologist and an Indian. The volume is studded with poems marked by emotional toughness and vigorous language, as well as a continuing concern for the lyric, as in "How I Came to be a Graduate Student":

> I am shut away without food
> in a house where all are dead
> when it looks like I may break loose
> they tell me I'm *moving* now and
> congratulations . . .
> . . . It's that kind
> of moving: from grave
> to grave.[5]

More than *Long Division,* however, *Academic Squaw* made it clear that Wendy Rose is not a monochromatic poet. As though the skill and breadth of sensibility evident in that second volume were not enough to establish her as a poet of consequence, she offers in this book poems on Chinatown, on becoming thirty, on being a woman, on her poetic craft, on other poets.

Even the way she handles a central resource of native writers, the assumption of one's cultural heritage, is mature. She could easily have employed conventional Hopi elements like so much poetic local color. Instead she probes them for points of personal relevance and then adapts, instead of adopts, them. "Walking on a Prayerstick" is a fine example of this.

In *Builder Kachina: A Home-Going Cycle* (1979), she returned to the small chapbook, poem-cycle format to explore the common enough theme of going home as a spiritual as well as physical journey. Two things are particularly interesting about her treatment of this motif. First, in terms of her personal growth as a poet, this is not only her most sustained single effort but also the most varied tonally, with moments of almost casual, vernacular narrative, incantatory and lyric song, and wry, even pungent humor, all orchestrated toward an unusual end. Although journey themes conventionally conclude with the discovery of, or failure to discover, the object of one's quest, neither of these endings is possible for Rose. She is at once both Hopi and, as an urban Indian from her childhood, non-Hopi. "California moves my pen," she writes, "but Hotevilla [her father's Hopi village] dashes through my blood."[6] She cannot legitimately inherit that which has never been accessible to her, the Hopi culture, and yet she cannot reclaim that which, in a sense, she has never lost, her family and emotional ties to Hopi. In one poem in the previous volume, *Academic Squaw,* she had asked: "Is there / a Katcina for / people like me?"[7] Kachinas are supernatural beings the Hopis believe are responsible for managing all the forces in the world. The fact that she and other urbanized, displaced Indians exist suggests to her that there must be a guardian responsible for them. In the last poem in *Builder Kachina* she hears her father say, "We'll build your roots," and looks up to see Builder Kachina standing next to her. The Hopis, however, do not have such a kachina. What Rose has done, in one bold stroke, is to appropriate the principle at the heart of Hopi religion to her own personal situation, inventing a kachina to answer the question asked in the previous volume.

All of these poems, and many new ones, were collected in *Lost Copper* (1981), which is organized along the theme of reintegration of self, beginning with poems from *Long Division,* moving through poems from *Academic Squaw* and poems about important relationships in her life, and concluding with *Builder Kachina.* Of all the native poets now writing, none, with the possible exception of Momaday, has more consistently reasserted the creation of personal identity through art.

Irony even more intense than that of Rose courses through the poetry of James Welch (Blackfeet/Gros Ventre), whose novels are discussed in the previous chapter. His only book of poetry to date, *Riding the Earthboy 40* (1970), shows many of the stylistic marks and the thematic preoccupations that appear in his fiction. Life on the Earthboy 40, a forty-acre quarter section of Montana range land, is presented with the same grim humor and lean picturing of the High Plains landscape familiar from his novel *Winter in the Blood.* The surrealistic emphasis on dreaming, wordplay, and the juxtaposition of radically different images immediately recalls *The Death of Jim Loney.* Welch has acknowledged the influence of several poets, especially the South American surrealists Borges, Vallejo, and Neruda, and his friend the late James Wright.[8] But the work bears Welch's stamp. Perhaps no one has written about this part of the country from such an acute angle of vision since Stephen Crane.

The comparison with Crane is not gratuitous. Welch consistently uses color to establish tonal correlatives to emotional states, especially blue in all its numbing and debilitating iciness, pale blue suggesting the heartless infinities of a winter sky, blue purpling to the color of death. Often he deliberately mixes levels of diction, jarring the reader from the posture of nobility with a sudden colloquialism, an equivalent in vocabulary of his absurdist vision. He can use brutal understatement to point up the absurdity of familiar pieties: "The wages of sin is to live where / the mountains give down to the Indian town."[9] In poems like "Dreaming Winter" and "Magic Fox" the density of the texture is so great that one enters into the world of dream-speech and must carefully work through a constellation of images, as in the poetry of James Wright, in order to become present to the motivating vision. In "Magic Fox" we are witness to the power of beauty over the imagination. Dark, greening, richly sensual, exhilarating, the sexuality of the young girl "not yet twenty-four, / but blonde as morning birds" enchants the men and sets them like foxes on the scent of her beauty. Yet her beauty is only for them in their imagination, and they turn, foxes like dreaming dogs, in the urgent nightmares of their sleep.

Most of the time James Welch moves through an absurd, hard-bitten world, one in which the weight of history, especially the burden of ancient animosities between whites and Indians, rests heavily on the land. Welch will not deny the truth of this, although he hates it. Of the noble savage, he urges us to "tell the mad decaying creep / we miss him. We never / meant it."[10] Nostalgia can never overcome the visible pain of the present, of "the three young bucks who shot the grocery up, / locked themselves in and cried for days, we're rich, / help us, oh God, we're rich."[11] In this absurd world, mute old men and sullen young ones stagger toward different, but equally small, fires, the first for memory, the second for anger and anticipated revenge.

It is too easy to mistake Welch's subject, however, as Indians who "once imitated life," too easy to emphasize only the force of circumstance measured in the weight of the successive, stressed syllables in the opening line of "Surviving": "The day long cold hard rain drove . . . ."[12] But in that poem the Indian narrator as witness prevents such a simple interpretation. The same is true in "Thanksgiving at Snake Butte," when the poet and his companion in the course of a "holiday" ride "in this, their season of loss" come across a petroglyph carved by their ancestors. Something is gone, yes, a way of life, an easiness and comfortable acceptance of norms one sets for oneself, a social order of one's own making, but Indians have not disappeared. If the oral tradition remains only "something of honor and passion" to be begged from elders gathered around a weak wood stove in a forty-below night, yet it does remain. It is a matter of vision, more than faith, and of a thin but persistent memory: "look away and we are gone. / Look back. Tracks are there, a little faint. . . ."[13]

It is this persistence of memory in the face of knowledge, of vision in the face of blindness, that nourishes both rage and hope in Welch's world. Together he and his friends compose a "steady demolition team" whose business it is to explode the complacency of a nation that ignores the consequences of history or assigns them to reservations. "Any day," we are reminded, "we will crawl out to settle / old scores or create new roles, our masks / glittering in a comic rain."[14] It is a theme that needs more room than the lyric can provide, which turned Welch eventually to fiction.

The lyric is well suited, however, to the brief encounters with wonder, the momentary temptations to despair of Jim Barnes (Choctaw). *The American Book of the Dead* (1982) is patterned on the ancient Egyptian funerary classic, but epigraphs by and allusions to John Berryman, Dylan Thomas, Emerson, Aeschylus, Eliot, and Dante stake out the more familiar boundaries of the intellectual world from which Barnes departs. Indeed, leaving is the central metaphor in this book, not just leaving one town for the next but leaving—in the Egyptian sense—one world for the next. The principal theme is the evanescence of life, the awareness of losing a hold on the present and slipping into a past of memories or a future of dream, from either of which the poet must awake with a heightened awareness of his otherness, of "the ache / of aging in my living breath" (99).[15]

The volume opens with a poem from a cycle titled "Autobiography," about leaving Summerfield, a town whose sterile desiccation gives the lie

to its name. The poet knows, however, that even in leaving he will be
compelled to return "when the years have made / the town quick with old
men's dreams" (3). On the road, the poet becomes the archetypal wander-
er-observer, distanced enough from communities like Marshalltown, Iowa,
to observe grimly: "Christ would like / hanging here / . . . a town / to
leave your sins in, / from where every road / goes up" (71–72). But he is
also unflinchingly honest, and knows by the tremors in his own being that
"You could go mad here except for needs." Nowhere is the burden of this
act of identification more powerfully felt than in the section entitled
"Death by Water." By virtue of that title, drowning must here carry some
of Eliot's connotations of death by immersion in the flesh. So seductive is
drowning, "the lovliest / of deaths by far" (30), that he himself is tempted, but pulls back at the brink, vowing that "I will not drown / to know
my own life." Everywhere about him a stinking mortality dons the false
face of gentle sleep and sweet dreams. But that does not fool the Indians
and loggers of Grande Ronde, Oregon, who huddle in desperation beneath
Spirit Mountain. There he saw that the struggle for meaning and the
struggle for being were the same:

> There's not one soul left in this town
> who does not try to pray the frown
> off the stone face the mountain's made
> of: give us this day, god knows we've paid.
>   (65)

The wanderer's last poem, as expected, preaches nothing new, but "coming home again."

Although the cloak of mortality drapes itself heavily around his shoulders, it is Barnes's struggle to affirm his deliberate being in spite of that
burden that dominates this volume. While contemporary wisemen garner
applause philosophizing about the necessity of despair and decay, Barnes
rejoices in having "a bad mind that boils / in anger against the rot . . . it
coils / will spring, be sprung (who cares?), not rot" (91). We care, of
course, because he does. The maturity of his vision and the richness of his
language command our assent.

Duane McGinnis Niatum (Klallam) has written half a dozen volumes of
poetry, including three major collections. Like Momaday, Niatum reflects
in his poetry interests fostered by his advanced education, doing homage
to artists like Redon, Matisse, and Chagall, poets like Auden, Hugo,
Bishop, and Bogan. Like Rose he seeks to recover the tribal cultural context from which he is alienated.

Niatum's work revolves around three recurrent themes. The largest number of poems, especially in *Ascending Red Cedar Moon* (1973), detail his wanderings through the emotional badlands of sexual encounters, of love lost and found, frequently employing symbolist and imagist techniques to establish correlatives to emotional states. Most of these poems, and a good many of the others, employ a melancholy falling rhythm or adopt a studied contemplative pose. Neither the studied quality of the pose nor the tenuousness of the language of flowers and colors sufficiently distances his voice from his feelings to save most of these poems from pathos.

A second group of poems, many appearing in *Digging Out the Roots* (1977), are concerned with psychologically negotiating his relationship to his Irish father and his Klallam grandfather. In the end he accepts the advice of Salmon Berry Woman, "A gift from a recent dream. 'Your father,' she said, / 'Leave him in owl's cave, without light, shadow.' "[16] However successful Niatum has been in disengaging himself from that figure of his drunk, drowned father, the effort was a necessary one for Niatum, providing the motivation not only for his subsequent interpersonal relations but for his reclamation of his Klallam past. This is the subject of his third group of poems. In "The Sixties, No. 4," the poet and a lover, "Hoping Eros guide[d] fools through the maze, / . . . create[d] their own mythology in bed."[17] The search for his Klallam past is the subliminal reflection of this interiorized quest for meaning. In "No One Remembers Abandoning the Village of White Fir," he imagines himself to be a Klallam child asleep. This condition enables him to present an imagined unconscious, which he carries off initially with success: "Winds then clacked like bone rattles, / Shaking lost meters from the dark. / Many salmon still swim the rapid dreams / Of those children left alone with bluejay and chipmunk."[18] But in the third part of the poem, mythological figures like Coyote and Seatco step forward too deliberately and the blur of dream is lost for the clarity of a consciously assumed persona.

For the most part this is not Niatum's way. The sea, the gulls, berries, cedars, shamans, wolves, salmons, bears, smoke, and all the other cultural symbols of Northwest Coast tribal life, even native language words, are invoked almost as talismans, touchstones of a deep and private affective memory. In his later work, the chapbook pieces and some of the poems from *Digging Out the Roots,* he tries his hand at adopting a second-person or third-person mask. Combined with a tougher language and a shorter, often fragmented line, these personae sufficiently distance him from his experience to treat it ironically. Thus displaced from his private self, his poetry can be more easily shared and honored.

Songs from the Earth

A number of native poets have focused their attention on their relationship to the land. This is not a pastoral poetry, however, but a poetry deeply rooted in those aspects of the natural world, which have particular cultural significance. Often these cultural symbols derive from the particular tribal mythological context that is part of the poet's inheritance. The equation of the earth with man's flesh, a theme in Simon Ortiz's poetry, is a basic principle in the Emergence myth (see chapter 1) of Ortiz's Acoma community. The strawberries that play such an important role in Maurice Kenny's poetry are Iroquoian symbols of vitality. Nature, in other words, is endowed with meanings derived from tribal cultures and should not be arbitrarily interpreted by analogies to Western pastoral traditions.

Many of these poets also pay explicit tribute to the oral tradition, employing the formal principle of creation as performance in their poetry. Leslie Silko deliberately draws upon tribal mythology as a mode of interpreting contemporary events. Peter Blue Cloud consciously adopts a storytelling posture, preferring· familiar language and narrative forms to western modes of poetic composition. Maurice Kenny openly adopts the rhythmic phrasing of tribal song for his poems, chanting or singing them in performance. Simon Ortiz does all three.

Through four books of poetry, the recurrent themes of Simon Ortiz (Acoma) have been the community of the land, the life of the earth's body, the tragedy of losing touch with that life, the search to recover and the struggle to retain its substantial exhilaration. Frequently his poems have a strong narrative thread and employ colloquial diction, even local variations in speech patterns, to capture the sense of place. In order to share his vision, especially with people who have never read poetry before, Ortiz consciously built upon his own admiration for the vernacular tradition in modern poetry from Whitman through Sandburg to the Beats.

Like many poets, Ortiz has formulated a sense of the nature of language. Because he comes from an oral culture, he is more concerned with language as uttered than language as visual sign. Words, then, are not objects, but deeds, acts with power to organize experience; they are at once a way of perceiving as much as a way of expressing. To use language is to experience oneself as being-in-the-world. In discussing the relationship of song to context, Ortiz wrote: "Language is more than just a group of words and more than just the technical relationship between sounds and words. Language is more than a functional mechanism. It is a spiritual energy that is available to all. It includes all of us and is not exclusively in the power of human beings—we are part of that power as human beings."[19]

The relationship that language actualizes is the unity of man with the earth, a unity first imaged in the Emergence myth (chapter 1), which tells how man originally appeared on the surface of the earth by coming out of her womb. The relationship, then, is genetic and not metaphorical. Man is of the same stuff as the earth. In many of Ortiz's poems, the more deeply layered image is the almost geologic sense of man, his great age and his kinship with the earth. Their history, like their flesh, is one, and yet there is no doubt about which is greater. In "Spreading Wings" the poet flies over northern Arizona, urging himself against the illusion provided by technology: "I am only one part / among many parts, / not a singular eagle." He considers the Hopi villages and the Navajo sacred mountains in their integral relation to the earth. He contrasts the meteor crater near Winslow, a famous tourist site and scene of enormous natural violence, with the humanly created violence of atomic weapons exploded at Los Alamos: "a big jolt, / flame and then silence, / just the clouds forming." Modern America's urgency for goods and services has clearcut the forests and stripmined the land, defacing it utterly, and yet from the air there is no doubt that earth will endure the "feeble clawings" of man's ego. At the same time, there is no doubt about the anger and hurt.

If this can be done to the earth, the poet seems to say, it can be done to people, without shame, as if from necessity. In *Fight Back: For the Sake of the People, For the Sake of the Land* (1980) most of the poems focus on the exploitation of Indian labor and Indian land at a place billed locally as the Grants, New Mexico, Mineral Belt, one of the richest uranium concentrations in the United States. Although there are a few songs in the volume, most of the poems are narratives that explore the ironies, tragedies, and small personal victories of the workers. "It was That Indian" tells about the town's, indeed the country's, momentary adulation of a Navajo man named Martinez who first brought the green ore out of the mountains. The town erected a statue to him and named a park after him and then exploited the fact that he was an Indian to excuse the industry and deflect Indian complaints about irradiated water.

What is true for man's relationship to the earth in the larger historical and social perspective is also true for individuals. The image that organizes the entire volume of *Going for the Rain* (1976) is the circular journey to make offerings to the *shiwanna*, or rain priest: Preparation, Leaving, Returning, The Rain Falls. The birth of the individual recapitulates the emergence of the people at the beginning of things, and death is a return to the earth, not for good, but to return again in the rain as *shiwanna*.

The need for connection, which is the experience of continuity in life despite apparent separation, is a theme to which Ortiz often returns. In "A

San Diego Poem: January-February 1973" the poet returns to the image of an airplane flight, but here as an instance of dissociation. Cut off from the earth and equally distanced from his fellow passengers, he is so isolated that when he is returned to earth, the airport's maze of underground tunnels totally disorients him. Although he knows he is in "someplace called America," that knowledge cannot overcome his fear and he melts into the walls of the tunnel to become a "silent burial." In "Travels in the South" and other poems, Ortiz rejoices in the discovery that there are Indians everywhere, a vast network of relationships that contrast strongly with the invisibility of Indians to the white world, highlighting this point with the comment that he found himself very busy "explaining who [he] wasn't" and with the Florida park ranger's remark: This place is noted for the Indians / that don't live here anymore."

From Sand Creek (1981) is a tonally unified cycle of forty-five intense lyric poems representing Ortiz's personal and the nation's collective quest to recover the felt truth of history buried under the High Plains grass. From the perspective of a VA Hospital in Colorado—Ortiz served in the army in the mid-1960s—he recalls the dawn attack of Col. John Chivington on the Cheyenne and Arapaho, who were peacefully encamped along Sand Creek under a United States flag presented to their chief, Black Kettle, by President Lincoln. Surrounded by veterans of three wars, the poet remembers that even then, in November 1864, the attack was understood to be a politically expedient show of strength and will against an invented enemy: 105 women and children and 28 men died that morning. Not only Indians, he knows, must count the cost of the American dream of westering.

From Sand Creek paints a vision of America that is immediate and personal through the use of lyric poems, many almost cinematic in their emphasis on color and glimpsed action. These Ortiz weaves into an epic tapestry of recurrent images and themes: blood, steel, grass, night, whirlpools, hands and throats, memory and dream. Ortiz himself has compared the form of the cycle to symphonic music, and the work does resemble Wagnerian opera in its coloration and use of leitmotifs, building around a central theme: "The axiom / would be the glory of America / at last, / no wastelands, / no forgiveness" (17). No single poem better conveys the madness of such a history than one in which the deep, still night of the hospital ward is pierced suddenly by a distant scream. Fearful souls, veterans of foreign wars, embattled nightmares, gather in the basement arming themselves against the dark: "They'll never know. / Indians stalk beyond the dike, / carefully measure the distance, / count their bullets"

(55). The terror of history, from Sand Creek to Vietnam, continues in dreams. The final victims are the conquerors themselves. No one wants to remember, but Ortiz insists that "Love should be answerable for. / The responsibility of being enjoined" (91). If America can embrace its past in love, it can transcend the horror for a future full of hope.

Another southwestern poet whose work reflects a felt kinship with the land is Leslie Silko, from Laguna, the sister pueblo of Simon Ortiz's Acoma. Although she is known primarily for her novel *Ceremony* (chapter 4), she has published a volume of poetry, *Laguna Woman* (1974), and several new poems have appeared in anthologies and in her recent collection of prose and poetry, *Storyteller* (1981). Many of her poems use natural elements like water, sunlight, and butterflies to celebrate human sexuality. "When Sun Comes to Riverwoman" images lovemaking by describing sun-warmed sand and swirling brown water stirred by human thighs. As vitally connotative as these images are in themselves, the poem also draws upon the common southwestern myth of a woman magically impregnated by the sun and by water, perhaps even while drawing water from the river. The Keresan heroine of this myth at Laguna is Kochininako or Yellow Woman. Many of Silko's poems and stories feature modern characters reliving her adventures.

This mythic consciousness, which perceives contemporary happenings as shadows of prototypical events, and which also embraces man-animal transformations as a mode of being, is an integral part of Silko's vision. In "Toe'osh: A Laguna Coyote Story," she unmasks the traditional Laguna figure in a number of modern situations touching upon tribal politics, Anglo-Indian relations, native religion, even a writers' conference. In "Bear Country," one of her most effective poems, she suggests that men are drawn into the mountains by the beautiful songs of the bears; subconsciously fleeing the ugliness of the urban world, they go to live with the bears and become permanently changed. After addressing the reader as an imagined hiker whose wife and sons wait near the car in the canyon below, she invites him, hauntingly: "Go ahead / turn around / see the shape / of your foot prints / in the sand."[20]

Both the sensuality and the mythic consciousness of animals combine in several stunning poems that use hunting as a metaphor for human relationships and death as a metaphor for sexual union. In poems like "Where Mountain Lion Laid Down With Deer" or "Deer Song" natural predator-prey relationships are endowed with love. After the chase, death is in truth a willed surrender. "You see, / I will go with you," the deer says to the hunter, "I will go with you / because you love me / while I die."[21] Hunt-

ing, many native peoples believe, is a cooperative act in which the animal
gives up her flesh to the hunter, who releases her soul through respectful
ritual so that it can return to the Keeper of Game to be born again in
another body. Loving, Silko suggests in these poems, is this kind of dying
and being reborn, a beautiful violence.

Another group of poets has taken up similar themes rooted in the wood-
ed, granite landscape of the northeast. Maurice Kenny (Mohawk) is well
known as an editor who has brought many native poets to prominence
through his Strawberry Press. He has been publishing poetry himself since
the 1950s and has become a poet of reputation. A series of recent books
draws upon his native heritage and its roots in the north country, beginning with *North: Poems from Home* (1977). Kenny sings of connections between the land and history, delighting in the smallest moments of being,
which disclose in their sudden beauty and grace the oneness of all living
things. This, he says, is "The First Rule": "stones must form a circle first
not a wall . . . words cannot be spoken first." In "Land" he celebrates the
resilience of the earth by shifting back and forth between the present moment and the early nineteenth century, when Madam de Feriet "gave her
French aristocratic manner / to a sign post at the edge of the country
road, / tangled now by yellow roses and purple vetch."

Many of Kenny's poems, "Mulleins," for example, take up the vigorous,
declamatory rhythms of Whitman, surging in waves to break upon the
most remote shores of his vision, encompassing all. Others are compelling,
incantatory songs that catch the ancient rhythms of the tongue when literature was uttered art. In *I Am the Sun* (1979), he uses the repetitive form
of Ghost Dance songs to commemorate the events of Wounded Knee in
1973, but the expanding circle of chant ripples outward from that one
event, that one nation to urge upon all the renewal of faith and the restoration of the dream.

Kenny writes from his Brooklyn address in *Dancing Back Strong the Nation* (1979), invoking the past again to deal consciously with the urgency
of his displacement. The volume is about going home, more pointedly,
going "home from Brooklyn to the reservation / that was not home."[22]
There he is aware of the distance he measures in his feelings, "when the
tongue is not always on the handshake / when the dance is not on the
feet."[23] But neither is returning to Brooklyn from the reservation a returning home. Instead he eats woody strawberries, picked by foreign hands in
another land, while the blood reminds him of his youth when he ate "blood
berries that brought laughter . . . wild berries with their juices running /
down the roots of our mouths and our joy."[24] The urban landscape also is

the backdrop for much of *Kneading the Blood* (1981). Kenny's most recent book retains the visual power of his earlier work and its celebratory tone, but incantatory rhythms have given way to an honoring of silence. Here the spaces between the words are full of implication, and the words themselves, cast in more formal diction, constitute a language pulled up short to become conscious of itself and the moment. Each word, each line then, breathes a pause in holiness, honoring the dead who live in their being so honored: "we dropped you into dust / among marigolds" and "we barely knew the ticking of your clock / the weather of your dreams / the smell of your curse / the taint of your sin."[25] Hawks dominate the images of this volume, multivalent symbols of brute grace and the wonder of dying, of even the most anonymous person's nobility, of a transformation devoutly to be wished. Even death, especially death, Kenny seems to say, testifies to the vitality of the earth, which sways my praise.

Another Mohawk poet, Peter Blue Cloud, has published two books of poetry. *Turtle, Bear and Wolf* (1976), with a foreword by his friend Gary Snyder, is made up of several pieces whose rhythms move with the full chordal structure of organ music, swelling like a river to encompass the flow of images drawn from the natural world of the forest. Others adopt a surrealist perspective, like "Ochre Iron," which uses the renowned Mohawk domain of high steel as a background to elaborate a series of transformations about the loss of a father and personal stability as falling from the structure that collapses in the end. These losses weigh heavily elsewhere in the volume, as in "To-ta Ti-om," about one of his aunts, an herbal medicine woman whose presence and reverence for the earth were brought home to him in the aromas, the textures of the "feeling and smelling and tasting" that filled the seasons of her life. The volume concludes with a three-poem sequence, each poem named after one of the clan totems of the Mohawk nation. "Turtle" draws upon the origin story of the world built on a turtle's back. "Bear" sings the dance of continuance because despite death a Bear people arise. "Wolf" affirms the power of kinship, even though he is the object of all the energies of extinction, the insistent survivor.

Another long dramatic production, which he characterizes as a "play for voices," is the title poem of Blue Cloud's second volume, *White Corn Sister* (1979). The poem is based on the Iroquoian story of how corn came to the people in the person of a young girl and as a dream answered. Dreaming is very important to Iroquoian peoples as a principle of explanation and causation and needs to be lived out, to become history. In this story, corn is the answer to many dreams: the hunter's dream of hunger relieved; the medicine man's dream of sickness cured and evil defeated; the clan mother's dream of individuals formed into a community. After an apocalyptic middle section, which foretells the violent struggle between the polar forces of good and evil represented by the Rival Twins (see chapter 1: The Earth-Diver), an age of renewal is forecast, the appearance of which announces the end of the poem and the volume.

Like Blue Cloud and Kenny, Joseph Bruchac (Abenaki) has published several books of poetry that search out the Indian heritage of the northeast. Of these the most satisfying is *Entering Onandaga* (1979), a collection of memories, encounters with the landscape of stone, elm, and rivulet, of voices echoing in the ears of time: the "wirr and burp" of a chainsaw, the turn of speech of elders ("When you speak english / with the memory / of a first tongue / still sweet in your throat / it comes out different").[26] In other volumes Bruchac has explored Algonquian mythology and teaching state prison inmates to write poetry. Bruchac also translates poetry into English and edits the *Greenfield Review*.

The Visionary Poets

Few poets are truly visionary, capable of developing entire systems of personal symbols in response to the inner need to create alternate contexts of meaning. Both Ray Young Bear and Joy Harjo are moving in this direction, the first from an uneasy surrealism and the second from an evident dissatisfaction with irony. Both seem to have dropped not only Western conventions but tribal ones in search of a new synthesis that can account for the multiplicity of voices within.

The poetry of Ray Young Bear (Mesquakie) haunts the imagination. Collected in his first volume, *Winter of the Salamander* (1980), are songs and narratives built from the stuff of dreams. Motifs recur like siren songs throughout the volume: men in the bodies of cows, boys with the faces of fish, rivers of water surging through the ice bearing the burden of memory down to the ocean, houses with walls made of yesterday's voices. These he weaves together in simple, conversational diction that can erupt at any moment into vision, all without the slightest shift in temper. This is living, he suggests, a constant act of attention to the voices in the air, the water, the woods about us. Although he can find himself groping for colloquial relevance, he is strongest, clearest, most chilling in presenting us with these visions, fully realized yet so distanced by the impersonal voice that we are caught up in the dreaming, seduced into a terrible beauty.

"From his Dream" is an instance of such seductive storytelling. In this poem, a woman sits in her cold living room trapped by winter and by fear.

Her son has been out hunting all day, not cause for alarm in itself because he is a good hunter and knowledgeable of all possible dangers. As the father sets out to find him, he remembers a dream

> he had that morning of giant fish
> and coral snakes submerged in the icy waters
> of a river he had never seen,
> he and his son cornering a small horse
> covered with fish scales, bearing
> the head of a frightened man.
> its thin legs and cracked hooves. [27]

As he continues on his way he thinks no more about it. Toward evening he returns home, assuming his son has probably done the same. Crossing the river on the way home, crawling for fear of the thin ice, something tugs at his will and he turns his head from the far shore to look through the clear, bubbled ice beneath him, where "he saw the severed head of his son, / the hoof from his dream, / bouncing along the sandy bottom."

Not all of Young Bear's poems have this narrative coherence, but all share the concern for dream and its power to create a ground of significance for everyday life as real and as tangible as the external world itself. It is a reality we seldom see, and tragedy is the border between the two worlds:

> I see the lights
> in the eyes of the dwarfs. After
> the alcoholics have passed out
> in their cars, the dwarfs come out
> from the ditches. They brush their
> moist hands against the alcoholics'
> shiny faces. [28]

Another poem entitled "celebration" affirms the sacredness of life by offering glimpses of powwows, dancing, medicine and peyote rituals, while "at home, away from / the celebration, / a girl inserts herself / with a clothes hanger, / smears her guilt on the windows" (81).

In a third poem he addresses the tribal context as part of that matrix of meaning in the person of an elder who often finds himself called upon not only to preside over clan feasts and naming ceremonies but also "to speak / to the charred mouths of young / bodies that had died drunk." More "puzzled" than horrified at the deaths, he senses the incongruity of praying for an afterlife for a suicide who does not want any more life, while the mourners in his community are in fact asking him to affirm that "last dream, / the grandfather of all / dreams."[29]

Living, then, becomes a constant act of discernment, seeking after the wellsprings of meaning that spill into the present moment. Never an easy task, it is also often a dangerous one, for it can raise doubts about our authenticity so acute as to paralyze us, eventually eroding our belief in the possibility of any meaning at all.

In "it is the fish-faced boy who struggles," point of view shifts several times, from an exterior description of a boy sitting in the back of a wagon crossing an iron bridge, to his interior journey, which comes into being as a story of the boy's entry into the underwater world of the fish. From that moment on his remaining days at his family's fishing camp are colored by the brief experience of kinship with the hunted. This strongly contrasts with his experience in the bureaucracy of a hospital, where the host of a program on the television in his room preaching the need to preserve endangered species is interrupted by a doctor who asks permission to throw away his removed lung with the other hospital garbage. Such brutal juxtapositions bring us to the brink of faith and leave "our mind, an open wound." In drawing a picture of a person driven into isolation by experiences such as these, he is reminded of a "rotten frog"

> who had somehow lived through the night
> with half its body spread over
> the hot sunlit highway
> moss from the swamps
> entangled itself to the lower
> exposed organs and fibrous tissues
> assorted insects flew about
> and the frog blinked at each
> passing car.[30]

In this desperate state men seem small, frail, crushed creatures, pawns of fear as much as of fate.

The power of these poems is that in his several encounters with Badger, the mask of Death, Young Bear refuses to turn away. Instead, "knowing that a covenant with his spirit / is always too much to ask for" (90), he chooses to live and to bear into being as poetry the pain of a wounded humanity and to seek in visions a way beyond absurdity.

A similar motivation is moving Joy Harjo (Creek) along the same path. Many of the poems in her first book, *What Moon Drove Me to This?* (1979), provide a sympathetic but gritty commentary on contemporary Indian life.

Kansas City "coyotes" in "point-toe boots bought for a dollar down" run the bars in Tulsa or Oklahoma City, Chicago or Albuquerque, "drinking back the distance / before the long night / of the hunt," while their "angry women are building houses of stones / . . . grinding the mortar / between straw-thin teeth / and broken families."[31] This fragile world of chance meetings, conscious abandonments, and frail relationships brings her home quickly to herself and her sense of her own contingency.

Much of her poetry employs sun and moon imagery to explore cycles of fulfillment and abandonment, alternate realities and identities. Her fulfillment is found in union with the sun, in the roundness of the sun rising with life: "rising / the sun / the woman / bending and stretching / with the strength of her child / that moved in her belly."[32] The moon represents all that the sun does not: loneliness, failed relationships, the night world of her other self, the persona she calls Noni Daylight, who cruises bars and rides the highway's edge at ninety miles an hour. "The full moon," she writes, "is a good excuse for anything."[33] Yet it is not so simple, for the moon is often addressed in an almost sisterly manner and consoles her in her isolation, even though its presence is almost always a signal of defeated hopes. The sun, on the other hand, must wear an aura of guilt for being occasionally associated with the lover who has fled.

The emergence of the Noni Daylight persona opened to Harjo a new way of looking at herself and at human consciousness: "I think that there are other worlds going on at the same time, but because we have limited our vision of what the world is, we can't see them. . . . There's an inner landscape and an outer landscape. . . . I think you can go as far inward, and it's like you're extending outward too, like there are galaxies and planets [within] and that there is no limit."[34] Images of violent eruptions, of breaking in through the sky, of collisions, of borders crossed and boundaries violated, and of traveling great distances dominate this poetry of interior exploration as the poet takes conscious possession of the inner universe. At times her imagery can become too private, but at her best the energy generated by this journeying creates a powerful sense of identity that incorporates everything into the poetic self, so that finally she can speak for all the earth. As she asserts in "For Alva Benson, and for all those who have learned to speak," speaking is an act of giving birth, and the mother is a poet:

> And we go on, keep giving birth and watch
> ourselves die, over and over.
> And the ground spinning beneath us
> goes on talking.[35]

In this moment she finds her fulfillment both as woman and as poet, bringing into being her vision and her voices.

A Multitude of Voices

It is impossible to account for all the poets now writing, but a brief look at a few others may suggest some thematic and stylistic concerns different from those discussed above.

Several poets, including Joy Harjo and Wendy Rose, are becoming increasingly interested in their identity as women and the ways in which traditional native values enculturated in reservation upbringing offer models of being woman that are different from those of Anglo-American culture. This seems to be the direction in which much of the poetry of Linda Hogan and Paula Gunn Allen is moving.

Like that of her sister, Carol Lee Sanchez, the poetry of Paula Gunn Allen (Laguna/Sioux) grew out of experiences in San Francisco in middle and late 1960s. The fragmented syntax and abruptly broken images of her early work, like that in *Coyote's Daylight Trip* (1978), document her search for self among the ruins of experience. Poems like "Tucson: The First Night" and "Hanging Out in America" hint at a recovery of her tribal past and an emerging feminist identity. The volume's concluding poem, "Grandmother," evokes the Laguna mythical figure of Thought-Woman or Spider Woman, Maker of the World. In 1981 she published *Star Child,* which charged the language of urban self-explorers, potential burnout cases, and spiritual suicides, with the energies of compassion and loss. This is especially true in the title poem and in the sequence addressed to her students, "Christmas at Votech High, Santa Fe."

But the return to the source begun in the early work is poetically justified by the work in *A Cannon Between the Knees* (1981). Rooted in her native Southwest, the volume is more reflective, more mature, more unified in tone and theme, than previous work. Several poems, like "Womanwork" the "The Beautiful Woman Who Sings," celebrate native women as the source of connections, the focus of relationships, the well of creativity. But Allen also recognizes others, abandoned, caught, lonely, repressed, and bears witness to them in the cycle "Suicid/ing(ed) Indian Women." The chill portrait of a woman without hope is offered in "III/Delilah/Navajo," and the cycle ends with a poetic reflection on the prophetic Laguna myth of Corn Woman, who was sent away long ago by men who preferred gambling to their responsibilities, who "put women out of the center."

Also deeply concerned with her identity as a woman is Linda Hogan (Chickasaw). Her first book, *Calling Myself Home* (1978), centers on remembering as an act of love. The opening poem, "Turtle," transforms dreaming into a waking to consciousness of women who, with the shells of ages on their backs, can "see the years / back through his [turtle's] eyes."[36] In the languid rhythms of dream speech and the discontinuity of associated images, she suggests the transformation of persons not only into animals but into aspects of the earth such as trees, clay, and sedimentary rock. She personifies the ambiguity of her state's name—Oklahoma is a Choctaw word that can mean both "red earth" and "red people"—in the image of a potter whose fingers absorbed the red clay from their impress upon the shape emerging at his wheel. But she also knows that her tribal name means "they left as a tribe not a very great while ago" and adds, "they are always leaving, those people."[37] In that poem she bears witness to having to carry her heritage, her earth, her family entirely in her body. As the ambiguity of the title marvelously suggests, without a home she longs for one, to call herself back to Oklahoma and that past, but she realizes that in the end she can only, like the turtle, call her self home.

In *Daughters, I Love You* (1981) she continues to explore many of these themes under the shadow of a mushrooming pillar of fire, writing poetry in the face of nuclear holocaust. Less protest than plea, the many strong poems in this volume again exploit ironies of transformation: that light should be a sign of death and moral darkness; that mothers should be mourners giving birth to the doomed; that invention is destruction. The most potent irony: that all that women have come to symbolize for her— the earth, the future, the bond of shared humanity, the promise of continuance as a species—should be jeopardized in the name scrawled on the fuselage of the Hiroshima-bound B-29; "The Enola Gay, / was named for the pilot's mother."[38]

Another Oklahoma poet, Lance Henson (Cheyenne), has published several books of poetry that work the lyric minimalist vein. In *Naming the Dark* (1976), *Mistah* (1977), and *Buffalo Marrow on Black* (1981), Henson strives to capture the compelling images of memory and probe the layers of the unconscious. A pure imagist, he evokes the trembling silences of a soul intimate with its own loneliness in glimpses of old ladies in black shawls calling for their cats, of lovers alone before each other beneath a chill moon, of the distant barking of dogs and the wind moving among the trees down along the river in the night. A few poems move beyond these evening winter tonalities, populated by ghosts, measured by their absences, to take up specifically Cheyenne themes, pay homage to religious figures, recall historic events. But Henson seems most at ease in the presence of just one other, "each of us alone / tying our words / to the / dark."[39]

Another group of poets from widely divergent backgrounds and of varying abilities seem linked by the decision to create an often sardonic tone through the use of urban vernacular. They take a wry look at Indian bars and the powwow circuit, reservation suicides, and "one-eye'd Fords." Their growing number includes Carter Revard, Barney Bush, Janet Campbell Hale, nila northSun, Adrian Louis, and Diane Burns.

And new writers are emerging. Among those who have yet to publish a volume of poetry are Charles Ballard (Quapaw/Cherokee), Lew Blockolski (Cherokee/Choctaw), Grey Cohoe (Navajo), Anita Endrezze-Danielson (Yaqui), Louise Erdrich (Turtle Mountain Chippewa), Nia Francisco (Navajo), Patty L. Harjo/Ya-Ka-Nez (Seneca/Seminole), King D. Kuka (Blackfeet), Harold Littlebird (Santo Domingo/Laguna), Alonso Lopez (Papago), Phil Minthorn (Nez Percé/Cayuse), Thomas Peacock (Anishinabe), Liz Sohappy (Yakima), Jim Tollerud (Makah), Anna Walters (Pawnee/Oto), Roberta Hill Whiteman (Oneida), and Ramona Wilson (Colville). Some will certainly be embarking on an emphemeral career, but others will discipline themselves, grow in their craft, and become mature poets.

Chapter Six
Looking Sunward

Previous chapters have remarked only upon the main lines of development in Native American literature, but the resources available to the present generation of native writers are taking them into newer areas where they are just beginning to make their mark. A few of these branches, however, are sufficiently developed to deserve some examination.

One is a strong, emerging vein of nonfictional prose. Vine Deloria, Jr. (Sioux), stirred considerable national interest with the publication of *Custer Died for Your Sins* (1969). His witty, acerbic style quickly made him a popular commentator on Indian interests: "Into each life, it is said, some rain must fall. Some people have bad horoscopes, others take tips on the stock market. McNamara created the TFX and the Edsel . . . Indians have anthropologists."[1] If the sweeping generalizations of his broad editorial style often rested on factual inaccuracies or doubtful premises, it seemed enough that they communicated contemporary attitudes and realities with vigor and energy. Of his half a dozen other books, perhaps only *God Is Red* (1973) is of equal importance. In it, Deloria, himself the son of an Episcopal priest, excoriates Christianity and, like Eastman before him, offers a generalized Native American tribal religion as an alternative. Paula Gunn Allen (Laguna/Sioux) has begun writing criticism along similar lines, arguing in "The Sacred Hoop" that European and American literary criticism, like Christianity, begins with premises that are not consonant with the interests of Native American writing. Native American literature, however, has not developed a counterpart to the Black Aesthetic Movement of the 1960s and 1970s, perhaps because the pluralism implicit in the Native American tribal experience precludes any homogeneity.

N. Scott Momaday is breaking new ground with his intensely personal, poetic narratives, which essay the principal dilemma of an urbanized, thoroughly acculturated Indian: how to retain continuity with one's cultural heritage though displaced from the community that sustains it. The very structures of these works express the dynamic by which the psyche internalizes the mythic, historical, and cultural components of identity. *The Names* (1976) is a series of poetic reflections upon the meaning and emotional tenor of important experiences in the past. Confronting a photograph, he can re-create the dialogue of the dead and conjure up mannerisms for those he never knew, because the issue is not at all who the "names" in his past were in themselves, but who they are to him. "An idea of one's ancestry and posterity is really an idea of the self," he wrote. "I was formulating an idea of myself."[2] If such intense self-consciousness does occasionally produce a precious prose, it also gives rise to some of Momaday's finest writing, especially his descriptive passages of the southern Plains landscape.

In *The Way to Rainy Mountain* (1969) Momaday finds in autobiography a microcosm of the Kiowa cultural and historical experience. Moved by the death of his grandmother Aho, he journies from the Kiowa place of emergence in the mountain fastness of Yellowstone down to their Oklahoma reservation. It was, he wrote, "a whole journey, intricate with motion and meaning; and it is made with the whole memory, that experience of the mind which is legendary as well as historical, personal as well as cultural."[3] This journey comprises the narrative thrust of the work, which is articulated in three voices: the mythic, the historical-cultural, and the personal. In each vignette of the journey narrative, these voices are presented in different type faces and carefully arranged so that the personal and historical-cultural passages face the mythic one, speaking in a kind of a dialogue. In the first part, "Setting Out," the Kiowa are given their name, a way of seeing that is visionary, a way of speaking that is powerful, and a destiny as the people of Tai-me. In "Going On," the second part, Momaday offers a number of instances of continuity in value and custom between the first gifts given to the Kiowa and their historical experience. In the final part, "The Closing In," Momaday bears witness to the passing of the horse culture. But by inserting family history in the place taken by Kiowa myth in previous parts, he acknowledges that, in the person of his grandfather Mammedaty, the values and vision that made the Kiowa a distinctive people in a former era have been successfully internalized in the collective memory of his family and passed down to him in the present generation.

Contemporary native dramatists approach the issue of identity from a different tack, following the path of the first native dramatist, Lynn Riggs (Cherokee), who is—as pointed out in the discussion of his poetry—perhaps best known today as the author of *Green Grow the Lilacs* (1930), which was made into the musical *Oklahoma!* One of his plays, however, deals directly with Indians. *The Cherokee Night* (1936) is a series of scenes spanning thirty years and focused around Claremore Mound, the heart of the land. The characters are principally acculturated Indians whose lack of moral values is directly proportionate to the degree to which they emulate white behavior. Preoccupied with money, violent, and spiritually desolate, they stalk a landscape that has no meaning for them, epitomized by their refusal to trust to the magic of the arrowheads that Old Man Talbert, who has been visited by the spirits of the Cherokee dead, has taken from the Mound. Talbert knows them for what they are, "Muck and scum! . . . Dribbles of men and women! . . . You're dead, you ain't no good! Night's come on you."[4] The last scene of the play places historical responsibility for this condition on the invasion of Indian Territory by whites in the mid-nineteenth century.

Hanay Geiogamah (Kiowa), who helped organize the Native American Theatre Ensemble in 1972, has written, produced, and published three plays.[5] *Foghorn* is a brutal satire, each scene of which violently unmasks the psychic forces mobilized by conventional Anglo stereotypes of Indians: Pocahontas explains to her giggling companions the circumstances surrounding John Smith's blubbering apologies for his failure at love-making; the Lone Ranger calls Tonto his "faithful Injun companion" once too often and gets his throat cut. Framed by scenes of the Alcatraz and Wounded Knee occupations, the play dramatizes the need for native peoples to break the Anglo-forged ideological chains that bar them from their future. In *Body Indian,* a crippled Indian, Bobby Lee, winds up in a drinking party where his friends roll him for his money every time the wine he is drinking puts him to sleep. Although he had hoped to use the money, which he received from leasing his allotment, to pay for an alcohol rehabilitation program, he is less angry than numb. He realizes that there was no malicious intent in his friends' actions, that in fact they are so deeply in need of the community of the present that any future, his or theirs, is inconceivable to them. The most richly textured of Geiogamah's works is *49,* a play named after the post-powwow round of drinking-and-singing communality that inevitably trails off into early morning. Juxtaposed against the contemporary 49 session, which is being surrounded by highway police, are scenes in which figures representing the traditional past speak to the need for solidarity among the tribes and continuity of traditional values in spite of external changes. When, at the end of the play, the police try to drive the young people off the powwow grounds, the latter unite to form a solid front of dignity and pride to resist the dispersal of their emerging community and the silencing of their song.

The closing scene of *49* is a good image on which to conclude. Conclude, but not summarize, for one does not sum up such a vast literature without paying a great price. In the haste to create a few meaningful generalizations—perhaps something about the importance of the land or attitudes toward language—the vitality and richness with which the cultural pluralism of Native America endows its literary record, the multiplicity of vibrant and particular voices, would be blurred, even muted. To some degree the constraints imposed upon this volume have already caused such distortion. There has been no space to discuss the humor of Will Rogers (Cherokee), the science fiction of Russell Bates (Cherokee), or the accomplishments of Indian journalism, and very little space for unnamed others whose poetry and fiction are only hinted at in the bibliography that follows. But let it rest. Better not to summarize rashly, to close the door quickly, but to leave it open and listen to the singing.

Notes and References

In order to conserve space, the following abbreviations are used in this section and in the Selected Bibliography: *AA, American Anthropologist; ARBAE* and *BBAE* for the *Annual Reports* and *Bulletins* of the Bureau of American Ethnology; *AMNH-B* and *AMNH-P* for the *Bulletins* and *Papers* of the American Museum of Natural History; *CO, Chronicles of Oklahoma; JAF, Journal of American Folklore; PAES, Publications of the American Ethnological Society;* and *RFTE, Report of the Fifth Thule Expedition.* In order to reduce the number of notes, in-text references have been used wherever possible. When either in-text references or notes for chapter 5 lack page numbers, they refer to unpaginated poetry chapbooks.

Chapter One

1. The prehistory of North America and ethnographic circumstances of tribal cultures are described in Robert F. Spencer, Jesse D. Jennings, et al., *The Native Americans* (New York: Harper & Row, 1963).

2. Knud Rasmussen, "The Iglulik Eskimo" *RFTE* 7, no. 1 (1930):229.

3. Richard Bauman, *Verbal Art as Performance* (Rowley, Mass.: Newberry House, 1978), p. 38ff. The description of performance throughout this paragraph follows Bauman.

4. Albert Lord, *The Singer of Tales* (Cambridge, Mass.: Harvard University Press, 1960), p. 124.

5. Judith Irvine, "Formality and Informality in Communicative Events," *AA* 81 (1979):773–90.

6. Alan Dundes, *The Morphology of North American Indian Folktales,* Folklore Fellows Communications, 195 (Helsinki, 1964).

7. Andrew Wiget, *The Oral Literatures of Native North America: A Critical Anthology* 2 vols. (Ph.D. diss. University of Utah, 1977) 1:86–87.

8. Gladys Reichard, "Literary Types and the Dissemination of Myths," *JAF* 34 (1914):274.

9. These stories can be found in J. O. Dorsey and A. L. Kroeber, "Traditions of the Arapahos," *Field Museum, Anthropology Series* 5 (1903); J. R. Swanton, "Tlingit Myths and Texts," *BBAE* 39 (1909); C. M. Barbeau, "Loucheux [Kutchin] Myths," *JAF* 28 (1915); Roland B. Dixon, "Maidu Myths," *AMNH-B7,* no. 2 (1902–7).

10. J. N. B. Hewitt, "Iroquoian Cosmology," *ARBAE* 21 (1903).

11. Reichard, "Literary Types." See also Stith Thompson, "The Star Husband," in Alan Dundes, *The Study of Folklore* (Englewood Cliffs, N.J.: Prentice-Hall, 1965), pp. 414–74.

12. Alanson Skinner and John V. Satterlee, "Folklore of the Menomini Indians," *AMNH-P* 13, no. 3 (1915). Also Laura Makarius, "The Crime of Manabozho," *AA* 75 (1973).

13. Clifford Geertz, "Religion as a Cultural System," in *The Interpretation of Cultures* (New York: Basic Books, 1973).

14. William Fenton, "This Island, the World on Turtle's Back," *JAF* 75 (1962):283–300.

15. Mircea Eliade, *Shamanism: Archaic Techniques of Ecstasy* (Princeton, N.J.: Princeton University Press, 1964), also Elli Kaija Köngas, "The Earth-Diver," *Ethnohistory* 7 (1960):151–80.

16. Jesse D. Jennings, ed., *Ancient Native Americans* (San Francisco: W. H. Freeman, 1978), pp. 256–58, 409–12.

17. Erminie Wheeler-Voegelin and R. W. Moore, "The Emergence Myth in Native America," *Indiana University Publications in Folklore* 9 (1957):66–91.

18. Donald Bahr, "On the Complexity of Southwestern Indian Emergence Myths," *Journal of Anthropological Research* 33 (1977):317–49.

19. I have based my paraphrases on Ruth Bunzel, "Zuni Origin Myths," *ARBAE* 47 (1930), and Washington Matthews, "Navaho Legends," *Memoirs of the American Folklore Society* 5 (1897).

20. Laura Thompson, "Logico-Aesthetic Integration in Hopi Culture," *AA* 47 (1945):540–53.

21. This and the preceding quotation from ibid., p. 541.

22. Adrian Recinos, *Popul Vuh: The Sacred Book of the Quiche Maya* (Norman: University of Oklahoma Press, 1950), and Miguel León-Portilla, *Pre-Columbian Literatures of Mexico* (Norman: University of Oklahoma Press, 1969).

23. Clyde Kluckhohn and Dorothea Leighton, *The Navaho* (Cambridge, Mass.: Harvard University Press, 1946), Chapter 9.

24. Robert Lowie, "Myths of the Crow Indians," *AMNH-P* 25 (1927):7.

25. The reader is directed to videotaped performances of Trickster narratives by Helen Sekaquaptewa (Hopi) and Rudolf Kane (White Mountain Apache), part of the series *Words and Place: Native Literature of the Southwest,* produced by Larry Evers (New York: Clearwater Publishing, 1981).

26. The following Winnebago stories all appear in Paul Radin, *The Trickster* (New York: Schocken, 1972).

27. Leonard Bloomfield, *Sacred Stories of the Sweetgrass Cree,* Bulletin 60, National Museum of Man (Ottawa, 1930).

28. Radin, *Trickster,* p. 136.

29. MacLinscott Ricketts, "The North American Indian Trickster," *History of Religions* 5 (1966):334.

30. Barbara Babcock-Abrahams, " 'A Tolerated Margin of Mess': The Trickster and His Tales Reconsidered," *Journal of the Folklore Institute* 9 (1975):147–86.

31. J. Barre Toelken, "The 'Pretty Language' of Yellowman: Genre, Mode and Texture in Navaho Coyote Narratives," *Genre* 2 (1969):221.

32. Bruce T. Grindal, "The Sisala Trickster," *JAF* 86 (1973):173–75.

33. Radin, *Trickster,* pp. 148–50.

34. Clifford Geertz, "The Impact of the Concept of Culture on the Concept of Man," in *The Interpretation of Cultures* (New York: Basic Books, 1973), pp. 46–47.

35. Ricketts, "Trickster," p. 343.

Chapter Two

1. Quoted in Ruth Bunzel, "Zuni Ritual Poetry," *ARBAE* 47 (1930):617.

2. C. W. Vanderwerth, *Indian Oratory* (New York: Ballantine, 1971), p. 81.

3. Donald Bahr, *Pima and Papago Ritual Oratory* (San Francisco: Indian Historian Press, 1975), pp. 6–7.

4. Gary Gossen, *Chamulas in the World of the Sun* (Cambridge, Mass.: Harvard University Press, 1974), pp. 48–49.

5. Thomas Jefferson, "Query VI," *Notes on the State of Virginia* (1787).

6. Edna Sorber, "The Noble Eloquent Savage," *Ethnohistory* 20 (1972):227–36.

7. Theodore J. Balgooyen, "The Plains Indian as Public Speaker," *Landmarks in Western Oratory,* ed. David H. Graves (Laramie: University of Wyoming Press, 1968), pp. 12–43.

8. Michael Foster, *From Earth to Beyond the Sky: An Ethnographic Approach to Four Iroquois Speech Events* (Ottawa: National Museum of Man, 1974), p. 7.

9. Ibid., chapter 5.

10. Ibid., p. 32ff.

11. See Vanderwerth, *Indian Oratory.*

12. Richard Ek, "Red Cloud's Cooper Union Address," *Central States Speech Journal* 17 (1966):260.

13. Vanderwerth, *Indian Oratory,* p. 37.

14. Frances Densmore, "Chippewa Music, I." *BBAE* 45 (1910):5–6.

15. Roland B. Dixon, *Maidu Texts,* Publications of the American Ethnological Society, 4 (Leyden: E. J. Brill, 1912), pp. 24–25.

16. On this crucial point, see Dan Ben-Amos, "Analytical Categories and Ethnic Genres," in his *Folklore Genres* (Austin: University of Texas Press, 1976).

17. Avram Yarmolinsky, "Aleutian Manuscript Collection," *Bulletin of the New York Public Library* 48, no. 3 (1944).

18. Frances Densmore, "Nootka and Quileute Music," *BBAE* 124 (1939):269.

19. Frances Densmore, "Teton Sioux Music," *BBAE* 61 (1918):371.

20. Ibid., p. 518.

21. Frances Densmore, "Papago Music," *BBAE* 90 (1929):187.

22. Knud Rasmussen, "The Netsilik Eskimo," *RFTE* 8, nos. 1, 2 (1931):321.

23. A. Grove Day, *The Sky Clears* (Lincoln: University of Nebraska Press, 1951), p. 43.

24. Helen H. Roberts and Diamond Jenness, *Songs of the Copper Eskimo*, Report of the Canadian Arctic Expedition, 1913–1918 (Ottawa: F. A. Acland, 1925), 14:504.

25. Rasmussen, "Netsilik," p. 321.

26. This conversation is reported in Miguel León-Portilla, *Pre-Columbian Literatures of Mexico* (Norman: University of Oklahoma Press, 1969), pp. 81–83.

27. Andrew Wiget, "Aztec Lyrics: Poetry in a World of Continually Perishing Flowers," *Latin American Indian Literatures* 4 (1980): 1–11.

28. Translated by Arthur J. O. Anderson, *Grammatical Examples, Exercises and Review for Use with Rules of the Aztec Language* (Salt Lake City: University of Utah Press, 1973), p. 135.

29. Knud Rasmussen, "The Intellectual Culture of the Caribou Eskimo," *RFTE* 7, no. 2 (1930):52, 54.

30. Morris E. Opler, "The Creative Role of Shamanism in Mescalero Apache Myth," *JAF* 50 (1946):269.

31. Ruth Bunzel, "Zuni Ritual Poetry," *ARBAE* 47 (1930):617, n. 1.

32. See the classic study by Arnold Van Gennep, *The Rites of Passage* (Chicago: University of Chicago Press, 1960).

33. Knud Rasmussen, *Across Arctic America* (New York: Putnam's, 1927), p. 24.

34. Densmore, "Nootka and Quileute Music," p. 226.

35. Charlotte Johnson Frisbie, *Kinaaldá: A Study of the Navajo Girl's Puberty Ceremony* (Middletown, Conn.: Wesleyan University Press, 1967), pp. 298–99.

36. Pliny Early Goddard, "Gotal—A Mescalero Apache Ceremony," *Putnam Anniversary Volume* (New York: G. E. Stechert, 1909), p. 386.

37. Leland C. Wyman, *The Windways of the Navaho* (Colorado Springs: Taylor Museum, 1962), pp. 173–79.

38. Ruth Underhill, *Red Man's Religion* (Chicago: University of Chicago Press, 1965), p. 84.

39. Frances Densmore, "Music of Santo Domingo Pueblo, New Mexico," *Papers of the Southwest Museum,* no. 12 (Los Angeles, 1938):68–69.

40. Franz Boas, "Ethnology of the Kwakiutl," *ARBAE* 35 (1921); Helen H. Roberts, "The First Salmon Ceremony of the Karok," *AA* 34 (1932):426–40.

41. Andrew Wiget, "Sayatasha's Night Chant: A Literary Textual Analysis of a Zuni Ritual Poem," *American Indian Culture and Research Journal* 4 (1980):99–140.

42. David Aberle, "The Peyote Religion among the Navajo," *Viking Fund Publications in Anthropology* 42 (1966):320–21.

43. Densmore, "Nootka and Quileute Music," p. 263.

44. Frances Densmore, "Chippewa Music, II" *BBAE* 53 (1913):79.

45. Rasmussen, The Iglulik Eskimo, pp. 122–23.

46. Densmore, "Teton Sioux Music," p. 180.

47. Ibid., p. 302.

48. Clark Wissler, "The Sun Dance of the Blackfoot," *AMNH-P* 16, no. 2 (1918):260.

49. Leslie Spier, "The Sun Dance of the Plains Indians: Its Development and Diffusion," *AMNH-P* 16, no. 7 (1921):461.

50. Joseph Jorgensen, *The Sun Dance Religion: Power for the Powerless* (Chicago: University of Chicago Press, 1972), p. 236.

51. Aberle, *Peyote Religion*, p. 319.

52. James Mooney, "The Ghost Dance Religion and the Sioux Outbreak of 1890," *ARBAE* 16, no. 2 (1896):641–1110.

53. Ibid., pp. 961, 967.

54. Ibid., p. 976.

55. Mircea Eliade, *The Sacred and the Profane* (New York: Harper & Row, 1961), pp. 94–95.

56. R. D. Theisz, ed., *Buckskin Tokens: Contemporary Oral Narratives of the Lakota* (Aberdeen, S.D.: North Plains Press, 1975). See Ofelia Zepeda, ed., *When It Rains: Papago and Pima Poetry* (Tucson: University of Arizona, Sun Tracks, 1982), for an example of contemporary poetry written in native language.

Chapter Three

1. The Walam Olum, with translation and commentary, is available in C. F. Voegelin et al,, *The Walam Olum or Red Score: The Migration Legend of the Lenni Lenape or Delaware Indians* (Indianapolis: Indiana Historical Society, 1954). The historical information in the following pages was drawn from Arrell Morgan Gibson, *The American Indian: Prehistory to the Present* (Lexington, Mass.: D. C. Heath, 1980).

2. Gibson, *American Indian*, p. 451.

3. Walter Meserve, "English Works of Seventeenth-Century Indians," *American Quarterly* 8 (1956):264–76.

4. Harold Blodgett, *Samson Occum: The Biography of an Indian Preacher* (Hanover, N.H.: Dartmouth College Publications, 1935), p. 35.

5. Ibid, p. 145.

6. William Apes, "Eulogy on King Philip," in Kim McQuaid, "William Apes, Pequot: An Indian Reformer in the Jackson Era," *New England Quarterly* 50 (1977):605–25.

7. William Apes, *A Son of the Forest* (New York: G. E. Bunce, 1831). Page references in text.

8. Arnold Krupat, "The Indian Autobiography: Origins, Type, and Function," *American Literature* 53 (1981):22–42. Quoted from p. 41.

9. Donald Jackson, ed., *Black Hawk, An Autobiography* (Urbana: University of Illinois Press, 1955), p. 41. Subsequent page references in text. Summaries

and full references for all biographies mentioned in this chapter can be found in H. David Brumble III, *An Annotated Bibliography of American Indian and Eskimo Autobiographies* (Lincoln: University of Nebraska Press, 1981), an excellent reference.

10. Charles Eastman, *From the Deep Woods to Civilization* (Boston: Little, Brown, 1916), p. 53.

11. Ibid., pp. 57–58.

12. Charles Eastman, *The Soul of the Indian* (Boston: Houghton Mifflin, 1911), p. 15.

13. Studies of Neihardt's collaboration include Sally McClusky, "*Black Elk Speaks,* and so does John Neihardt," *Western American Literature* 6 (1972):231–42, whence the subsequent Neihardt quotation is taken, and Carol T. Holly, "*Black Elk Speaks* and the Making of Indian Autobiography," *Genre* 12 (1979):117–36.

14. David Cusick, *A Sketch of the Ancient History of the Six Nations* (Lewiston, N.Y.: Author, 1827).

15. Leroy V. Eid, "The Ojibwa-Iroquois War: The War the Five Nations Did Not Win," *Ethnohistory* 26 (1979):297–324.

16. Many of these anthropologists were associated with the Bureau of American Ethnology and some discussion of their work can be found in Neil M. Judd, *The Bureau of American Ethnology* (Norman: University of Oklahoma Press, 1967).

17. The letter to Watie is quoted in Edward Everett Dale, "John Rollin Ridge," *CO* 4 (1926):312–21; letter on p. 319. See also Carolyn Thomas Foreman, "Edward Bushyhead and John Rollin Ridge, Cherokee Editors in California," *CO* (1936):295–301.

18. San Francisco: Henri Peyot, 1868. Pages references in text.

19. Topeka: Crane, 1910. Page references in text. For further biographical details see William Elsey Connelley, "Memoir of Alexander Lawrence Posey," in the same volume, pp. 5–65; Doris Challacombe, "Alexander Lawrence Posey," *CO* 11 (1933):1011–18; Alexander Posey, "Journal of the Creek Enrollment Field Party, 1905," *CO* 46 (1968):2–19; and Edward Everett Dale, "Journal of Alexander Posey with Annotation," *CO* 45 (1968):393–432.

20. See "E. Pauline Johnson," in Marion Gridley, *American Indian Women* (New York: Hawthorn Books, 1974), pp. 67–73.

21. Rpt. Don Mills (Ontario: Paperjacks, 1972). Page references in text.

22. Mount Pleasant, Ohio: Elisha Bates, 1823. Attribution to Boudinot in *National Union Catalogue, Pre-1956 Imprints,* vol. 69, p. 151. Page references in text. For a discussion of the *Phoenix* and other Indian journalism, see James E. Murphy and Sharon M. Murphy, *Let My People Know: American Indian Journalism, 1928–1978* (Norman: University of Oklahoma Press, 1981). See also Ralph H. Gabriel, *Elias Boudinot: Cherokee, and His America* (Norman: University of Oklahoma Press, 1941).

23. Rept. Norman: University of Oklahoma Press, 1955. Page references in text.

24. Alexander Posey, "Letter of Fus Fixico," *Vinita Chieftain* 5, no. 204 (June 6, 1903).

25. Posey, *Indian Journal,* Eufala, Oklahoma, June 26, 1903.

26. "John Oskison, 72, Wrote of Indians," obit., *New York Times,* February 27, 1947, p. 21. Publication dates of the stories are: "When the Grass Grew Long," *Century Magazine* 40 (1899): 247–49; "The Quality of Mercy," *Century Magazine* 46 (1899):178–81; "Young Henry and the Old Man," *McClure's* 31 (1908):237–39.

27. See "Gertrude Simmons Bonnin, A Modern Progressive," in Marion E. Gridley, *American Indian Women* (New York: Hawthorn Books, 1974), pp. 81–87, also Mary E. Young, "Gertrude Bonnin," *Notable American Women, 1607–1950: A Biographical Dictionary* (Cambridge, Mass.: Harvard-Belknap Press, 1971), pp. 198–200.

28. See Cecilia Bain Buechner, "The Pokagons," *Indiana Historical Society Publications* 10, no. 5 (Indianapolis, 1933):281–342; and David H. Dickason, "Chief Simon Pokagon: 'The Indian Longfellow,' " *Indiana Magazine of History* 57 (1961):127–40. Dickason attributes the quoted characterization of Pokagon at the end of the paragraph to Frederick Webb Hodge of the Bureau of American Ethnology; he also provides some discussion of *Queen of the Woods.*

Chapter Four

1. Arrell Gibson, *The American Indian: Prehistory to Present* (Lexington, Mass.: D. C. Heath, 1980), p. 513.

2. Dexter Fisher, "Introduction," *Cogewea, The Half-Blood* (1927; rpt. Lincoln: University of Nebraska, 1981).

3. For biographical reference, see chapter 3, n. 26.

4. Terry P. Wilson, "Osage Oxonian: The Heritage of John Joseph Mathews," *CO* 59 (1981):264–93. Page references to *Sundown* (rpt. Boston: Gregg Press, 1980) in text.

5. Wilson, p. 277.

6. Undoubtedly based on the "Osage Oil Murders," from 1921–24, during which over twenty people were killed so that oil rights would eventually accrue to and enrich a single person.

7. Charles Larson, *American Indian Fiction* (Albuquerque: University of New Mexico Press, 1978), p. 61.

8. This information from Lawrence Towner's "Introduction" to *The Surrounded* (1936; rpt. Albuquerque: University of New Mexico Press, 1964). All parenthetical citations from this edition.

9. Material in this section drawn from Gibson, *American Indian.*

10. Ibid., p. 552.

11. For a brief discussion of Momaday's autobiographical works see chapter 6. Parenthetical page references to *House Made of Dawn* use the Perennial paper-

back edition (New York: Harper & Row, 1971). Some useful perspectives on the novel are Carol Oleson, "The Remembered Earth: Momaday's *House Made of Dawn*," *South Dakota Review* 11 (1973):59–78; and H. S. McAllister, "Incarnate Grace and the Paths of Salvation in *House Made of Dawn*," *South Dakota Review* 12 (1974–75):115–25.

12. Evers's article is the essential reading: "Words and Place: A Reading of *House Made of Dawn*," *Western American Literature* 11 (1977):297–320.

13. This quotation, from Momaday's oft-reprinted essay "The Man Made of Words," can be found in Geary Hobson's fine anthology *The Remembered Earth* (1979; rpt. Albuquerque: University of New Mexico Press, 1981), p. 162.

14. Biographical information from a sketch in *Laguna Woman* (Greenfield Center, N.Y.: Greenfield Review Press, 1974) and from *Storyteller* (New York: Seaver Books, 1981).

15. The edition used for page citations in the text is the Signet paperback edition (New York: New American Library, 1978).

16. Elaine Jahner, "An Interview with Leslie Marmon Silko," *Book Forum* 5 (1981):386.

17. Ortiz's story appears in Ken Rosen, *The Man to Send Rain Clouds* (New York: Vintage, 1974), and also in Ortiz's collection *The Howbah Indians* (Tucson: Blue Moon Press, 1979).

18. The editions used herein for page references in the text are *Winter in the Blood* (New York: Bantam, 1975) and *The Death of Jim Loney* (New York: Harper & Row Perennial, 1981).

19. D'Arcy McNickle, *Wind From an Enemy Sky* (New York: Harper & Row, 1978). Page references in text.

20. See Rupert Costo, "*Seven Arrows* Desecrates Cheyenne," *Indian Historian* 5, no. 2 (Summer 1972), and Vine Deloria's response, "The Cheyenne Experience," *Natural History*, November 1972.

21. Gerald Vizenor, *Darkness in St. Louis Bearheart* (St. Paul, Minn.: Truck Press, 1978). Page references in text.

22. Gerald Vizenor, *Wordarrows* (Minneapolis: University of Minnesota Press, 1978).

23. Alan Velie, "Beyond the Novel Chippewa Style: Gerald Vizenor's Post-Modern Fiction," in *Four American Indian Literary Masters* (Norman: University of Oklahoma Press, 1982), p. 136.

Chapter Five

1. N. Scott Momaday, "A Conversation with N. Scott Momaday," *Sun Tracks* 2, no. 2 (1976):18–21.

2. "The Gourd Dance: The Giveaway," in *The Gourd Dancer* (New York: Harper & Row, 1976), p. 37.

3. Wendy Rose, "The Anthropology Convention," in *Long Division: A*

Tribal History (New York: Strawberry Press, 1976), n.p. (see headnote).

4. Wendy Rose, "Long Division: A Tribal History," in *Long Division.*

5. Wendy Rose, "How I Came to Be a Graduate Student," in *Academic Squaw: Reports to the World from the Ivory Tower* (Marvin, S.D.: Blue Cloud Quarterly Press, 1978).

6. Wendy Rose, "Builder Kachina: Going Home," in *Builder Kachina: A Home-Going Cycle* (Marvin, S.D.: Blue Cloud Quarterly Press, 1979).

7. Wendy Rose, "Dancing with the New Kachina," in *Academic Squaw.*

8. See Alan Velie, "Blackfeet Surrealism: The Poetry of James Welch," in *Four American Indian Literary Masters* (Norman: University of Oklahoma Press, 1982), pp. 67–90.

9. James Welch, "The Last Priest Didn't Even Say Goodbye," in *Riding the Earthboy 40* (New York: Harper & Row, 1970). Subsequently identified as *Riding.*

10. James Welch, "Directions to the Nomad," in *Riding,* p. 13.

11. James Welch, "Harlem, Montana: Just Off the Reservation," in *Riding,* p. 31.

12. James Welch, "The Only Bar in Dixon" and "Surviving," in *Riding,* pp. 39, 46.

13. James Welch, "Blackfeet, Blood and Piegan," in *Riding,* p. 36.

14. James Welch, "Never Give a Bum an Even Break," in *Riding,* p. 71.

15. Jim Barnes, *The American Book of the Dead* (Urbana: University of Illinois Press, 1982). Page references in text.

16. Duane Niatum. "In New York City," in *Digging Out Roots* (New York: Harper & Row, 1977), p. 34.

17. Duane Niatum, "The Sixties, No. 4" in *Ascending Red Cedar Moon* (New York: Harper & Row, 1973), p. 43.

18. Duane Niatum, "No One Remembers Abandoning the Village of White Firs," in *Ascending,* p. 5.

19. Simon Ortiz, "Song: Poetry and Language," *Sun Tracks* 3, no. 2 (1977):9–12.

20. Leslie Silko, "Story from Bear Country," in *The Remembered Earth,* ed. Geary Hobson (Albuquerque: University of New Mexico Press, 1981), p. 216.

21. Leslie Silko, "Where Mountain Lion Lay Down With Deer," in *Voices of the Rainbow* (New York: Viking, 1975), p. 14.

22. Maurice Kenny, "Going Home," in *Dancing Back Strong The Nation* (Marvin, S.D.: Blue Cloud Quarterly Press, 1979).

23. Maurice Kenny, "North in Winter," in *Dancing.*

24. Maurice Kenny, "Wild Strawberries," in *Dancing.*

25. Maurice Kenny, "The Parts We Keep," in *Kneading the Blood* (New York: Strawberry Press, 1981).

26. Joseph Bruchac, "November at Onandaga," in *Entering Onandaga* (Austin, Tex.: Cold Mountain Press, 1978), p. 16.

27. Ray Young Bear, "From That Dream," in *Winter of the Salamander* (New York: Harper & Row, 1980), pp. 86–87. Hereafter identified as *Winter.*

28. Ray Young Bear, "It Seems as If We Are So Far Apart," in *Winter,* p. 130.

29. Ray Young Bear, "The Last Dream," in *Winter,* p. 89.

30. Ray Young Bear, "Three Reasons for Transgression: The Fierce Head of the Eagle, the Otter and the Daylight," in *Winter,* p. 200.

31. Joy Harjo, *What Moon Drove Me to This?* (New York: Ishmael Reed Books, 1979), pp. 15, 6, 18. Hereafter identified as *Moon*.

32. Joy Harjo, "Early Morning Woman," in *Moon,* p. 3.

33. Joy Harjo, "Looking Back," in *Moon,* P. 54.

34. Interview with Joy Harjo, Dartmouth College, April 7, 1981.

35. "For Alva Benson, and For Those Who Have Learned to Speak," in *She Had Some Horses* (New York: Thunder's Mouth Press, 1983), p. 19.

36. Linda Hogan, "Turtle," in *Calling Myself Home* (Greenfield Center, N.Y.: Greenfield Review Press, 1978), p. 3.

37. Linda Hogan, "Blessing," in *Calling Myself Home,* p. 27.

38. Linda Hogan, "X-Ray of My Daughter," in *Daughters, I Love You* (Denver: Loretto Heights College, 1981), p. 10.

39. Lance Henson, "Rune," in *Mistah* (New York: Strawberry Press, 1977).

Chapter Six

1. Vine Deloria, Jr., *Custer Died For Your Sins* (New York: Macmillan, 1969), p. 78.

2. N. Scott Momaday, *The Names: A Memoir* (New York: Harper & Row, 1976), p. 97.

3. N. Scott Momaday, *The Way to Rainy Mountain* (Albuquerque: University of New Mexico Press, 1969), p. 4.

4. Lynn Riggs, *The Cherokee Night* (New York: Samuel French, 1936), p. 152.

5. These are collected in *New Native American Drama: Three Plays* (Norman: University of Oklahoma Press, 1980).

Selected Bibliography

The primary and secondary literature associated with Native America is vast. A solid introductory historical survey is Arrell Gibson's *The American Indian: Prehistory to Present* (Lexington, Mass.: Heath, 1980), which can be complemented by Alvin Josephy's *The Indian Heritage of America* (New York: Bantam, 1968) and Angie Debo's *A History of the Indians of the United States* (Norman: University of Oklahoma Press, 1970). Harold Driver's survey of cultures, *Indians of North America* (Chicago: University of Chicago Press, 1961), should be supplemented with the new *Handbook of American Indians* (Washington, D.C.: Smithsonian Institution, 1978–), projected for fifteen volumes, each covering a different culture area; six volumes have been published already. This replaces the older *Handbook of American Indians, BBAE* 39 (1907–10). The principal reference work is Murdock and O'Leary's bibliography (see below), but also see the Newberry Library's series of tribal and topical bibliographies. Biographical information can be found in

Dockstader, Frederick J. (Oneida). *Great North American Indians: Profiles in Life and Leadership.* New York: Van Nostrand, 1977.
Gridley, Marion E. *Indians of Today.* Chicago: Indian Council Fire, 1936, rpt. 1960.
——— ——. *American Indian Women.* New York: Hawthorn, 1974.
Liberty, Margot, ed. *American Indian Intellectuals.* St. Paul, Minn.: West, 1978. The 1976 proceedings of the American Ethnological Society.

PRIMARY SOURCES

1. Poetry
Allen, Paula Gunn (Laguna/Sioux). *Star Child.* Marvin, S.D.: Blue Cloud Quarterly Press, 1980.
———. *A Cannon between the Knees.* New York: Contact II Press, 1981.
Arnett, Caroll/Gogisgi (Cherokee). *Tsalagi.* New Rochelle, N.J.: Elizabeth Press, 1976.
Barnes, Jim (Choctaw). *The American Book of the Dead.* Urbana: University of Illinois Press, 1982.
Blue Cloud, Peter/Aroniawenrate (Mohawk). *Turtle, Bear and Wolf.* Mohawk Nation at Rooseveltown, N.Y.: Akwesasne Notes, 1976.
Bruchac, Joseph (Abenaki). *Entering Onanadaga.* Austin, Tex.: Cold Mountain Press, 1978.

Burns, Diane (Anishinabe). *Riding the One-Eyed Ford.* New York: Contact II Publications, 1981.

Cardiff, Gladys (Cherokee). *To Frighten a Storm.* Port Townsend, Wash.: Copper Canyon Press, 1976.

Conley, Robert J. (Cherokee). *Adawosgi, Swimmer Wesley Snell: A Cherokee Memorial.* Marvin, S.D.: Blue Cloud Quarterly Press, 1980.

Hale, Janet Campbell (Coeur d'Alene). *Custer Lives in Humboldt County.* Greenfield Center, N.Y.: Greenfield Review Press, 1978.

Harjo, Joy (Creek). *What Moon Drove Me To This?* Berkeley: Reed & Cannon, 1978.

Henson, Lance (Cheyenne). *Naming the Dark.* Norman, Okla.: Point Riders Press, 1976.

————. *Buffalo Marrow on Black.* Edmond, Okla.: Full Count Press, 1981.

Hogan, Linda (Chickasaw). *Calling Myself Home.* Greenfield Center, N.Y.: Greenfield Review Press, 1978.

————. *Daughters, I Love You.* Denver, Col.: Loretto Heights College, Women's Center, 1981.

Johnson, E. Pauline (Mohawk). *Flint and Feather.* 1917, rpt. Don Mills, Ontario: Paperjacks, 1972.

Kenny, Maurice (Mohawk). *North: Poems from Home.* Marvin, S.D.: Blue Cloud Quarterly, 1977.

————. *Kneading the Blood.* New York: Strawberry Press, 1980.

————. *Blackrobe.* Saranac Lake, N.Y.: North Country Community College Press, 1982.

Momaday, N. Scott (Kiowa). *The Gourd Dancer: Poems.* New York: Harper & Row, 1976.

Niatum, Duane McGinnis (Klallam). *Digging Out the Roots.* New York: Harper & Row, 1977.

————. *Songs for the Harvester of Dreams.* Seattle: University of Washington Press, 1981.

Ortiz, Simon (Acoma). *Going for the Rain.* New York: Harper & Row, 1976.

————. *From Sand Creek.* New York: Thunder's Mouth Press, 1981.

Posey, Alexander (Creek). *The Poems of Alexander Lawrence Posey.* Topeka: Crane, 1910.

Revard, Carter (Osage). *Ponca War Dancers.* Norman, Okla. Point Riders Press, 1981.

Ridge, John Rollin (Cherokee). *Poems.* San Francisco: Henri Payot, 1868.

Riggs, Lynn (Cherokee). *The Iron Dish.* Garden City, N.Y.: Doubleday, Doran, 1930.

Rose, Wendy (Hopi/Miwok). *Long Division: A Tribal History.* New York: Strawberry Press, 1976.

————. *Lost Copper.* Morongo Indian Reservation: Malki Museum Press, 1980.

Salisbury, Ralph (Cherokee). *Spirit Beast Chant.* Marvin, S.D.: Blue Cloud Quarterly Press, 1982.

Silko, Leslie (Laguna). *Laguna Woman.* Greenfield Center, N.Y.: Greenfield Review Press, 1974.

Walsh, Marnie (Sioux). *A Taste of the Knife.* Boise: Ahsahta Press, 1976.

Welch, James (Blackfeet/Gros Ventre). *Riding the Earthboy 40.* New York: Harper & Row, 1970.

Young Bear, Ray A. (Mesquakie). *Winter of the Salamander.* New York: Harper & Row, 1980.

2. Fiction

Bradford, Denton R. (Minsee). *Tsali.* San Francisco: Indian Historian Press, 1972. Novel.

Bruchac, Joseph (Abenaki). *The Dreams of Jesse Brown.* Austin, Tex.: Cold Mountain Press, 1978. Novel.

Chief Eagle, Dallas (Sioux). *Winter Count.* Colorado Springs: Denton-Berkeland Printing Co., 1967. Novel.

Eastman, Charles A./Ohiyesa (Sioux). *Red Hunters and Animal People.* New York: Harper & Brothers, 1904. Short fiction.

————. *Old Indian Days.* New York: McClure, 1907. Short fiction.

————. *Smoky Day's Wigwam Evenings: Indian Stories Retold.* With Elaine G. Eastman. Boston: Little, Brown, 1909. Short fiction.

Geiogamah, Hanay (Kiowa). *New Native American Drama: Three Plays* ["Foghorn," "49," and "Body Indian"]. Norman: University of Oklahoma Press, 1980.

Griffis, Joseph K./Chief Tahan (Osage). *Indian Circle Stories.* Burlington, Vt: Free Press Printing Co., 1928. Short fiction.

Hale, Janet Campbell (Coeur d'Alene). *The Owl's Song.* New York: Avon, 1976. Novel.

King, Bruce. *Dustoff.* Santa Fe: Institute of American Indian Art, 1982. Drama.

Mathews, John Joseph (Osage). *Sundown.* New York: Longmans, Green, 1934, rpt Boston: G. K. Hall–Gregg Press, 1980. Novel.

McNickle, D'Arcy (Salish). *Runner in the Sun.* New York: Holt, Rinehart & Winston, 1954. Novel.

————. *The Surrounded.* 1936, rpt. 1978. Albuquerque: University of New Mexico Press. Novel.

————. *Wind From an Enemy Sky.* New York: Harper & Row, 1978. Novel.

Momaday, N. Scott (Kiowa). *House Made of Dawn.* New York: Harper & Row, 1966. Novel.

————. *The Way to Rainy Mountain.* Albuquerque: University of New Mexico Press, 1969.

Mourning Dove/Humishima (Okanagon). *Co-Go-Wea, or the Half-Blood.* Caldwell, Idaho: Caxton Printers, 1927. Novel.

Ortiz, Simon (Acoma). *The Howbah Indians.* Tucson: Blue Moon Press, 1978. Short fiction.

Oskison, John Milton (Cherokee). *Wild Harvest.* New York: D. Appleton, 1925.
    Novel.
————. *Black Jack Davey.* New York: D. Appleton, 1926. Novel.
————. *Brothers Three.* New York: Macmillan, 1935. Novel.
Pierre, Chief George (Colville). *Autumn's Bounty.* San Antonio: Naylor, 1972.
    Novel.
Pokagon, Chief Simon (Potawatomi). *Queen of the Woods.* Hartford, Mich.: C. H.
    Engle, 1899, rpt. Berrian Springs, Mich. Hardscrabble Books, 1972.
    Novel.
Riggs, Lynn (Cherokee). *Green Grow the Lilacs.* New York: Samuel French, 1931.
    Drama.
————. *The Cherokee Night.* New York: Samuel French, 1936. Drama.
Rosen, Kenneth, ed. *The Man to Send Rainclouds: Contemporary Stories by American
    Indians.* New York: Viking, 1974. Short fiction by Silko, Ortiz, Popkes,
    Walters, Gorman.
Silko, Leslie Marmon (Laguna). *Ceremony.* New York: Viking, 1977. Novel.
————. *Storyteller.* New York: Seaver Books, 1981. Short fiction.
Storm, Hyemeyohsts (Cheyenne). *Seven Arrows.* New York: Harper & Row, 1972.
    Novel.
————. *The Song of Hyeyoehkah.* New York: Harper & Row, 1980. Novel.
Vizenor, Gerald (Anishinabe). *Darkness in St. Louis Bearheart.* St. Paul, Minn.:
    Truck Press, 1978. Novel.
Welch, James (Blackfeet). *Winter in the Blood.* New York: Harper & Row, 1974.
    Novel.
————. *The Death of Jim Loney.* New York: Harper & Row, 1979. Novel.
Zitkala-Sa/Gertrude Bonnin (Sioux). *Old Indian Legends.* Boston: Ginn and Com-
    pany, 1901. Short fiction
————. *American Indian Stories.* Washington, D.C.: Hayworth Publishing
    House, 1921. Short fiction.

3. Other Writings
Apes, William (Pequot). *A Son of the Forest: The Experience of William Apes, a Native
    of the Forest, Comprising a Notice of the Pequod Tribe of Indians, Written by Him-
    self.* New York: Author, 1829; New York: G. E. Bunce, 1831.
————. *Eulogy on King Philip, as Pronounced at the Oden, in Federal Street, Boston, by
    the Rev. William Apes, an Indian.* Boston: Author, 1836.
Blackbird, Andrew J./Macketebenessy (Ottawa). *History of the Ottawa and Chippe-
    wa Indians of Michigan; a Grammar of Theirr* [sic] *Language, and Personal and
    Family History of the Author.* 1887. Republished as *Complete Both Early and
    Late History of the Ottawa and Chippewa Indians.* 1897; rpt. Petosky, Mich.:
    Little Traverse Regional History Society, 1977.
Black Hawk (Sauk). *Black Hawk: An Autobiography.* Edited by J. A. Patterson.
    Cincinnati, 1833. Rpt. edited by Donald Jackson. Urbana: University of

Illinois Press, 1964.

[Boudinot, Elias]. *Poor Sarah, or Religion Exemplified in the Life and Death of an Indian Woman.* Mount Pleasant, Ohio: Elisha Bates, 1823.

Clarke, Peter Dooyentáte (Wyandotte). *Origin and Traditional History of the Wyandotts, and Sketches of Other Indian Tribes of North America: True Traditional Stories of Tecumseh and His League, in the Years 1811 and 1812.* Toronto: Hunter, Ross, 1870.

Copway, George (Ojibwa). *The Life, History, and Travels of Kah-ge-ga-gah-bowh (George Copway), a Young Indian Chief of the Ojebwa Nation, in Regard to Christianity and their Future Prospects.* Albany, N.Y.: Weed & Parsons, 1847; Philadelphia: James Harmstead, 1847. Rpt. as *The Life, Letters & Speeches of Kah-ge-ga-gah-bowh, or G. Copway.* New York: Benedict, 1850.

———. *The Traditional History and Characteristic Sketches of the Ojibway Nation.* London: Gilpin, 1850. Republished as *Indian Life and Indian History, by an Indian Author, Embracing the Traditions of the North American Indians Regarding Themselves, Particularly of That Most Important of All Tribes, The Ojebways.* 1858; rpt. New York: AMS, 1977.

Cusick, David (Tuscarora) *Sketches of Ancient History of the Six Nations . . . .* Lewiston, NY: Author, 1827. 2nd ed. Lockport, NY: Colley Lathrop, 1828.

Deloria, Ella (Sioux). *Dakota Texts.* Publications of the American Ethnological Society, 14. 1932; rpt. Vermillion, S.D.: Dakota Press, 1974.

Deloria, Vine, Jr. (Sioux). *Custer Died for Your Sins: An Indian Manifesto.* New York: Macmillan, 1969; New York: Avon, 1970.

———. *God Is Red.* New York: Grosset, 1973; New York: Macmillan, 1975; New York; Dell, 1975.

Eastman, Charles Alexander (Sioux). *Indian Boyhood.* New York: McClure, 1902, rpt. New York: Dover, 1971.

———. *The Soul of the Indian: An Interpretation.* Boston: Little, Brown, 1911, rpt. Lincoln: University of Nebraska Press, 1980.

———. *From the Deep Woods to Civilization.* Boston: Little, Brown, 1916.

Hewitt, John N. B. (Tuscarora), ed. *Iroquoian Cosmology, Part One (Two).* Annual Report of the Bureau of American Ethnology, 21 (43). Washington, D.C.: Government Printing Office, 1904 (1928).

Jacobs, Peter/Pahtahsega (Ojibwa). *Journal of the Reverend Peter Jacobs, Indian Wesleyan Missionary, from Rice to the Hudson's Bay Territory, and Returning. Commencing May 1852.* Toronto: Anson Gree, 1853; Boston: Rand, 1853.

Johnson, Elias (Tuscarora). *Legends, Traditions and Laws of the Iroquois or Six Nations, and History of the Tuscarora Indians.* 1881; rpt. New York: AMS, 1977.

Jones, Peter (Ojibwa). *History of the Ojibway Indians, With Especial Reference to Their Conversion to Christianity.* 1861.

Mathews, John Joseph (Osage). *Wah'Kon'Tah: The Osage and the White Man's Road.* Norman: University of Oklahoma Press, 1932, 1968.

———. *The Osages: Children of the Middle Waters.* 1961; rpt. Norman: University of Oklahoma Press, 1973.

McNickle, D'Arcy (Salish). *They Came Here First: The Epic of the American Indian.* 1949; rpt. New York: Octagon, 1975.

————. *Native American Tribalism: Indian Survivals and Renewals.* New York: Oxford University Press, 1973.

Mourning Dove/Humishuma; Cristal McLeod Galler (Okanogan). *Coyote Stories.* With notes by Lucullus Virgil McWhorter/Old Wolf. Foreword by Chief Standing Bear. Edited by Heister Dean Guie. 1933; rpt. New York: AMS, 1977.

————. *The Tales of the Okanogans.* Edited by Donald M. Hines. Fairfield, Wash. Ye Galleon, 1976, Flagstaff: Museum of Northern Arizona, 1954.

Occom, Samson (Mohegan). "A Sermon Preached at the Execution of Moses Paul. . . ." New Haven Conn. T. & S. Green, 1772.

————. *A Choice Collection of Hymns and Spiritual Songs Intented* [sic] *for the Edification of Sincere Christians of All Denominations.* London: Timothy Green, 1774.

Oskison, John Milton (Cherokee). *Tecumseh and His Times: The Story of a Great Indian.* New York: Putnam's 1938.

Parker, Arthur C. *Seneca Myths and Folktales.* Publications of the American Ethnological Society, 27. 1923.

Warren, William Whipple (Ojibwa). *History of the Ojibways, Based on Traditions and Oral Statements.* Collections of the Minnesota Historical Society, 5, 1885; rpt. Minneapolis: Ross & Haines, 1957.

Zitkala-Ša/Gertrude Simmons Bonnin (Sioux). "The Schooldays of an Indian Girl." *Atlantic Monthly,* February 1900, pp. 185–94.

————. "Why I Am a Pagan." *Atlantic Monthly,* December 1902, pp. 801–3.

4. Oral literature

Astrov, Margot. *American Indian Prose and Poetry.* New York: Capricorn, 1962.

Bahr, Donald. *Pima and Papago Ritual Oratory.* San Francisco: Indian Historian Press, 1975.

————. *Rainhouse and Ocean.* Flagstaff: Museum of Northern Arizona, 1979.

Bierhorst, John, ed. *Four Masterworks of American Indian Literature.* New York: Farrar, Strauss, & Giroux, 1974.

Curtis, Edward S. *The North American Indian.* 20 vols. Cambridge, Mass.: Norwood, 1908–30.

Curtis, Natalie. *The Indians' Book.* 1907, rpt. New York: Dover, 1968.

Day, A. Grove. *The Sky Clears.* Lincoln: University of Nebraska, 1951.

Evers, Larry, et al. *The South Corner of Time.* Tucson: University of Arizona Press (Sun Tracks), 1980.

Jacobs, Melville. *The Content and Style of an Oral Literature.* Chicago: University of Chicago Press, 1959.

Kilpatrick, Jack Frederick, and Kilpatrick, Anna. *Walk in Your Soul: Love Incantations of the Oklahoma Cherokee.* Dallas: Southern Methodist University Press, 1965.

León-Portilla, Miguel. *Pre-Columbian Literatures of Mexico.* Norman: University of Oklahoma Press, 1969.

Lowenstein, Tom, trans. *Eskimo Poems from Canada and Greenland.* Pittsburgh: University of Pittsburgh Press, 1973.

Nequatewa, Edmund. *The Truth of a Hopi.* 1936, rpt. Flagstaff: Northland Press, 1967.

Radin, Paul. *The Trickster.* 1956, rpt. New York: Schocken, 1972.

Ramsey, Jerold W. *Coyote Was Going There: Indian Literature of the Oregon Country.* Seattle: University of Washington Press, 1977.

Spinden, Herbert J. *Songs of the Tewa.* 1933, rpt. Santa Fe, N.M.: Sunstone Press, 1976.

Tedlock, Dennis. *Finding the Center.* New York: Dial, 1972.

Theisz, R. D., ed. *Buckskin Tokens: Contemporary Oral Narratives of the Lakota.* Aberdeen, S.D.: North Plains Press, 1975.

Thompson, Stith, ed. *Tales of the North American Indians.* 1929, rpt. Bloomington: Indiana University Press, 1966.

Underhill, Ruth M. *Singing for Power.* 1938, rpt. Berkeley: University of California Press, 1976.

Vanderwerth, W. C., ed. *Indian Oratory.* 1971, rpt. New York: Ballantine, 1975.

Wyman, Leland C. *Blessingway.* Tucson: University of Arizona Press, 1975.

5. Anthologies

Hobson, Geary, ed. *The Remembered Earth: An Anthology of Contemporary Native American Literature.* 1979, rpt. Albuquerque: University of New Mexico Press, 1981.

Milton, John R., ed. *The American Indian Speaks.* Vermillion, S.D.: Dakota Press, 1969.

Niatum, Duane, ed. *Carriers of the Dream Wheel: Contemporary Native American Poetry.* New York: Harper & Row, 1975.

Rosen, Kenneth, ed. *Voices of the Rainbow: Contemporary Poetry by American Indians.* New York: Seaver Books, 1975.

Turner, Frederick Jackson, III, ed. *The Portable North American Indian Reader.* New York: Viking, 1973.

SECONDARY SOURCES

1. Books and articles

Allen, Paula Gunn (Laguna/Sioux). "The Sacred Hoop: A Contemporary Indian Perspective on American Indian Literature." In Chapman, *Literature of the American Indians,* pp. 111–36. A perceptive essay by a leading Native American poet and critic.

———, ed. *Studies in American Indian Literature: Critical Essays and Course Designs.*

New York: Modern Language Association, 1983. Presents varied approaches to Native American literature, oral and written, with a useful section on resources.

Babcock-Abrahams, Barbara. " 'A Tolerated Margin of Mess' ": The Trickster and His Tales Reconsidered." *Journal of the Folklore Institute* 11 (1975):147–86. Good overview of possible interpretations and functions of this figure.

Boas, Franz. *Race, Language and Culture.* New York: Free Press, 1940. Contains over half a dozen important, even classic essays on native oral literatures.

Chapman, Abraham, ed. *Literature of the American Indians: Views and Interpretations.* New York: Macmillan-NAL, 1975. An early and very useful collection of essays.

Dundes, Alan. *The Morphology of North American Folktales.* Folklore Fellows Communications, 195. Helsinki: Suomalainen Tiedeakatemia, 1964. A difficult-to-find but valuable structural study of Native American myths, even more important for what it implies than what it demonstrates.

Evers, Larry. "Words and Place: A Reading of *House Made of Dawn.*" *Western American Literature* 11 (1977):297–320. The essential introduction to this difficult novel.

Frisbie, Charlotte J., ed. *Southwestern Indian Ritual Drama.* Albuquerque: University of New Mexico Press, 1981. Solid studies of ceremonials as "events" or ritual dramas.

Gill, Sam D. *Sacred Words: A Study of Navajo Religion and Prayer.* Westport, Conn.: Greenwood Press, 1981. A careful examination of the verbal art of Blessingway.

Gossen, Gary. *Chamulas in the World of the Sun.* Cambridge, Mass. Harvard University Press, 1974. The model study of the formal and aesthetic dimensions of a Native American (Mayan) oral literature.

Hymes, Dell. *"In Vain I Tried to Tell You": Essays in Native American Ethnopoetics.* Philadelphia: University of Pennsylvania Press, 1981. Essential; careful textual analysis combined with a useful and original methodological perspective.

Kroeber, Karl, ed. *Traditional Literatures of the American Indian: Texts and Interpretations.* Lincoln: University of Nebraska Press, 1981. Reprints expanded version of classic essay by Toelken as well as original criticism by Tedlock, Ramsey, Hymes, and the editor.

Larson, Charles R. *American Indian Fiction.* Albuquerque: University of New Mexico Press, 1978. Frequently incautious and thesis-bound; useful if handled with care.

Ramsey, Jarold W. "The Teacher of Modern American Indian Writing as Ethnographer and Critic." *College English* 41 (1979):163–69. Argument for balancing text and context.

———. "The Wife Who Goes Out Like a Man, Comes Back as a Hero: The Art of Two Oregon Indian Narratives." *PMLA* 92 (1977):9–18. Example of well-contextualized analysis illuminates meaning of native myths.

Reichard, Gladys A. "Individualism and Mythological Style." *JAF* 57 (1944):16–25. Good introduction to topic; antidote to notions of "communal authorship."

————. "Literary Types and Dissemination of Myths." *JAF* 34 (1921):269–307. Classic study of Earth-Diver myth; excellent example of folkloristic distribution study.

Ruoff, A. LaVonne Brown. "Ritual and Renewal: Keres Tradition in the Short Fiction of Leslie Silko." *MELUS* 5 (1978):2–17. Fine instance of this particular kind of source study.

Seyersted, Per. *Leslie Marmon Silko*. Western Writers Series Pamphlet, 45. Boise: Boise State University Press, 1980. A good overview, especially useful for short fiction.

Smith, William F., Jr. "American Indian Autobiographies." *American Indian Quarterly* 2 (1975):237–45. Surveys topic; examines several in some depth.

Swann, Brian, ed. *Smoothing the Ground: Essays on Native American Oral Literature.* Berkeley: University of California Press, 1983. An especially good selection of essays that features a judicious mix of pieces with broad theoretical interest and those focused on specific stories.

Tedlock, Dennis. "On the Translation of Style in Oral Narrative." *JAF* 84 (1971):114–33. Now a classic article, emphasizing the orality of verbal art.

————. "Pueblo Literature: Style and Verisimilitude." In Alfonso Ortiz, ed. *New Perspectives of the Pueblos*. Albuquerque: University of New Mexico Press, 1972, pp. 219–42. An analysis of Zuni aesthetic values revealed in legend.

————. *The Spoken Word and the Work of Interpretation*. Philadelphia: University of Pennsylvania Press, 1983. Collected essays, principally concerning Mayan and Zuni literatures, by a leading figure in oral literature studies.

Trimble, Martha S. *N. Scott Momaday*. Western Writers Series Pamphlet, 9. Boise: Boise State University Press, 1973. An early study of this major writer.

Velie, Alan R. *Four American Indian Literary Masters: N. Scott Momaday, James Welch, Leslie Marmon Silko and Gerald Vizenor*. Norman: University of Oklahoma Press, 1981. Useful essays on Welch's poetry and on Vizenor.

Waterman, T. T. "The Explanatory Element in the Folk-Tales of the North American Indians." *JAF* 27 (1914):1–54. Classic study on problems of reading myths as pseudoscientific explanations.

Wiget, Andrew O. "Sayatasha's Night Chant: A Literary Textual Analysis of a Zuni Ritual Poem." *American Indian Culture and Research Journal* 4 (1980):99–140. Multidisciplinary analysis of ritual poetry.

Special issue on *Winter in the Blood* (James Welch). *American Indian Quarterly* 4, no. 2 (1978).

Special issue on *Ceremony* (Leslie Silko). *American Indian Quarterly* 5, no. 1 (1979). Both contain invaluable collections of critical essays on these major works.

2. Bibliographies and indexes

Brumble, H. David, III. *An Annotated Bibliography of American Indian and Eskimo Autobiographies*. Lincoln: University of Nebraska Press, 1981. Indispensable for its thoroughness and useful annotations summarizing works. Well indexed.

Coffin, Tristram P. *Journal of American Folklore: Analytical Index for Volumes 1–70 (1888–1957)*. Philadelphia: American Folklore Society, 1958. Provides access to articles through tribe, motif and tale type, and genre.

Judd, Neil M. *The Bureau of American Ethnology*. Norman: University of Oklahoma Press, 1967. A list of all articles in the Annual Reports, Bulletins, and Anthropological Papers. Follows a useful history of the BAE.

Littlefield, Daniel F., Jr., and Parins, James W. *A Biobibliography of Native American Writers, 1772–1924*. Metuchen, N.J.: Scarecrow Press, 1981. Thorough search of Indian newspapers has made this an especially valuable tool. Required reading.

Murdock, George Peter, and O'Leary, Timothy. *Ethnographic Bibliography of North America*. 5 vols. New Haven: Human Relations Area Files, 1975. The essential bibliographic reference for cultural information.

Prucha, Francis Paul, S.J. *A Bibliographical Guide to Indian-White Relations in the United States*. Chicago: University of Chicago Press, 1977. Also supplement for works published from 1975–80 (Lincoln: University of Nebraska Press, 1982). Indexes articles on history, policy, and law, thus complementing Murdock and O'Leary.

Wiget, Andrew. "Sending a Voice: The Emergence of Contemporary Native American Poetry." *College English*, 46 (1984):598–609. Includes extensive bibliography.

Index